A PROGRAM FOR YOU

A PROGRAM FOR YOU

A Guide To
The Big Book's®*
Design For Living

 HAZELDEN®

*BIG BOOK is a registered trademark of Alcoholics Anonymous World Services, Inc.; used here with permission of AAWS.

First published April 1991.

ISBN: 0-89486-741-5

Library of Congress Catalog Card Number: 90-85763

Printed in the United States of America.

Hazelden Educational Materials offers a variety of information on chemical dependency and related areas. Our publications do not necessarily represent Hazelden's programs, nor do they officially speak for any Twelve Step organization.

The Twelve Steps and Twelve Traditions are reprinted and adapted with permission of Alcoholics Anonymous World Services, Inc. Permission to reprint and adapt the Twelve Steps does not mean that Alcoholics Anonymous has reviewed or approved the contents of this publication, nor that AA agrees with the views expressed herein. The views expressed herein are solely those of the authors. AA is a program of recovery from alcoholism. Use of the Twelve Steps in connection with programs and activities which are patterned after AA, but which address other problems, does not imply otherwise.

In the interest of fostering self-respect for each individual regardless of gender, the authors have alternated gender references in this book—switching from "he" to "she," and vice versa, in the examples given. The authors believe the issues of chemical dependency know no boundaries in regard to sex, creed, color, or religious affiliation.

Contents

Introduction—
How This Book Can Help

Alcoholics Anonymous, which is most often just called the Big Book, was first published in 1939. Since then it has sold millions of copies throughout the world and, for over six decades, has helped millions of people recover from alcoholism.

The two of us who wrote this book believe firmly that there are no better tools for recovery than the Big Book and the Twelve Steps that the Big Book offers and describes. We know this to be true in our lives, as well as in the lives of thousands of alcoholics we've met and talked with over the last three decades. We have also heard of thousands of more people with other addictions and compulsive behaviors who are finding that these same tools can change their lives.

The Big Book isn't hard to read; it's written in plain, everyday language, and every word of it is practical and down-to-earth. It's not a book of theory or philosophy. It offers a clear, step-by-step approach for your recovery. It enables you to really and fully understand the problem of alcohol addiction; it presents a clear, practical solution to the problem; and it shows you how to implement that solution in your own life through the Twelve Step program of action it describes.

Though the Big Book is easy to understand and follow from the first page to the last, we've found that lots of people have managed to misunderstand and misuse it. Some of them just skim parts of the book or skip over them entirely. Some start in the middle of the book instead of the beginning. Some people disregard or ignore some of the Twelve Steps. Others don't read the Big Book carefully, and they misunderstand or misinterpret what the authors are saying. Still others bring in all kinds of other ideas that aren't found anywhere in the Big Book. And some people in the

Alcoholics Anonymous fellowship and other Twelve Step programs haven't read the Big Book at all.

We think it's strange that the fellowship, as it has grown over the years, has gotten away from the very thing that it started with. But we see a great trend in the past few years of going back to the Big Book. We want to help that trend continue.

We've written this book for two reasons: first, to help people get everything out of the Big Book that we believe its author intended; and second, to bring people back to what we think the Big Book actually does for all of us who are in recovery. Because of the guidance of the Big Book and the grace of the Higher Power we've found through it, neither of us has found it necessary to take a drink in over twenty years. We want to help you understand for yourself what the Big Book really says, means, and can offer you. It doesn't matter whether you've been in the AA fellowship or other Twelve Step recovery groups for thirty years, two weeks, or not at all—the Big Book can enhance your life and your recovery. We've been studying and talking about the Big Book for most of our years of sobriety, and by now we've read it dozens of times. But every time we look at it we get more out of it.

You can use *A Program for You* by yourself, or as part of a Big Book study group of your own. All it takes to start a study group are two or more interested people, a copy of the Big Book, and a copy of *A Program for You.*

Ideally, we'd like you to read *Alcoholics Anonymous* from cover to cover, or at least through page 164, before you follow along using our book. If you prefer, though, you can just read a chapter or section of the Big Book at a time as we go through it with you. *But it's absolutely essential that at some point, you get a copy of the Big Book and read it carefully from the beginning to at least page 164.* We want to help you to understand the Big Book more thoroughly—we don't want to replace it! Be sure to read the book in the sequence in which it was written, and don't skim or skip over any sections. The

Big Book was put together in a certain way, and for you to get the most out of it, you need to use it in the way it was meant to be used.

Whenever we refer to a section or passage in the Big Book, we'll indicate what chapter, pages, and (when appropriate) lines we're talking about.*

A Program for You actually began not as a book, but as a workshop, and before that as a study group. Both of us had an interest in studying the Big Book for many years, and when we first met in 1973 we decided we'd get together regularly to study it. After a while, other people started asking if they could join us; we said sure, and pretty soon we had a group going. The group kept growing, people began to hear about us, and in 1977 a fellow in Oklahoma invited us to talk to the Alcoholics Anonymous group he was in. We did, and he made tapes of our talk. Pretty soon, copies of these tapes started making their way around the country.

And soon we were being regularly asked to do weekend workshops on the Big Book. We've done hundreds of them by now—in most major cities in the United States, and in many other parts of the world.

Both of us are members of the fellowship of Alcoholics Anonymous, but in writing this book we aren't speaking for anyone except ourselves. We don't consider ourselves to be the gurus of the Big Book, and we're not claiming to be experts on anything. We're just two old alcoholics who have studied the Big Book for a long time and want to share with others what we've learned. Feel free to agree or disagree with anything you read in this book. In fact, we recommend

---

*References to the Big Book are also listed in the margins beside the text where Big Book sections or passages are described. These references use the following abbreviations: "p." means *page*, and "pp." is *pages*; "l." means *line number*, and "ll." is *line numbers*. For example, the reference "p. 14, ll. 9-21" means page 14 of the Big Book, lines 9-21 on page 14. All references are from the third edition of the Big Book.

that you pay no attention to anything we say that can't be reconciled with the book *Alcoholics Anonymous,* since our purpose is to help you understand that book better.

The better you do understand the Big Book, the more it can help you in your own recovery. We hope that *A Program for You* will show you just how helpful the Big Book can be. We believe the Big Book can change your life just as dramatically as it did ours.

— THE AUTHORS

CHAPTER ONE

How It All Started

In order to really understand the Big Book—how it works, how it can transform our lives, and how to use it as a step-by-step program for recovery—we need to look at some of the history behind it. The "Foreword to Second Edition" (pages xv-xxi) contains a brief history, which you should read, but right now let's take a detailed look at some of the key people and the events that led up to the Big Book's publication.

Bill W. and Dr. Silkworth

It all began in Akron, Ohio in June 1935, during a talk between Bill W., a New York stockbroker and speculator, and Dr. Bob, an Akron physician. Both of these men were alcoholics. Dr. Bob was still having serious problems with alcohol, but Bill had stopped drinking six months earlier. He had been relieved of his obsession with alcohol by a sudden spiritual experience that occurred after meeting with a friend, Ebbie T., who had been in contact with the Oxford Groups of that day. The Oxford Groups were made up of people who sought to practice first-century Christianity, using their faith to help them overcome whatever problems they had. Bill W. had also been greatly helped by Dr. William D. Silkworth, a New York specialist in alcoholism, who nowadays is considered a medical saint by many Alcoholics Anonymous members. Dr. Silkworth's accounts appear on pages xxiii through xxx of the Big Book.

pp.xxiii-xxx

Like most alcoholics, Bill W. had had no idea what was wrong with him. He thought he suffered from a weak will or a lack of moral character. He also thought that his problem might boil down to sin—at least, this was something people had been telling him for years. But when Bill W. and Dr. Silkworth met, the doctor explained to him that he thought alcoholism was actually a disease—a twofold disease, both of the body and of the mind. He explained that Bill W. was allergic to alcohol, and that whenever Bill W. took a drink, it produced a physical craving for still more alcohol. This made it virtually impossible for Bill W. to stop drinking once he had started.

Dr. Silkworth also explained to Bill how the obsession for alcohol worked in alcoholics. Bill couldn't shake the idea that someday he'd be able to take a drink like other people. But the fact was that he would never be able to drink like non-alcoholics. Still, the hope and the idea that he could were so strong to Bill that it didn't matter how badly he wanted to stop drinking; his mind would always take him back to the idea of taking a drink, and he would believe that he could take a drink and be able to stop. So he'd have a drink, and the drink would trigger the allergy, and he wouldn't be able to keep himself from drinking some more.

Ebbie T.'s Experience of Recovery

Bill W. was fortunate in two ways. First, he may have been one of the first alcoholics who truly understood what his problem was. Second, he was lucky enough to be in contact with someone from the Oxford Groups, Ebbie T., who showed Bill a way to overcome the disease. Ebbie, an old drinking buddy of Bill's, had been an alcoholic for years. In fact, doctors had pronounced him incurable, and he had been on the verge of being locked up for alcoholic insanity. But then Ebbie had a vital spiritual experience that changed his life. As a result, he was sober.

Ebbie told Bill W. that a spiritual experience like the one he had had would be the solution to Bill's problem of alcohol addiction. Ebbie gave Bill a series of steps and guidelines from the Oxford Groups that formed a practical program of recovery. He probably told Bill something like this: "If you can apply this program to your life, have a spiritual experience of your own, and find a Power greater than any human power, you'll be able to recover from the disease of alcoholism."

So Bill W. learned three separate things at about the same time: (1) he got an accurate description of his problem from Dr. Silkworth; (2) he learned the solution to his problem from Ebbie; and (3) he got a practical program of action from the Oxford Groups, through Ebbie. He might have been the first human being to learn these three things together.

Bill W.'s Awakening and Recovery

Bill W. had a spiritual awakening of his own in November of 1934, shortly after meeting with Ebbie. This came to be known as Bill's "white flash" because it was such a sudden and dramatic experience—a flood of light bringing a great peace and confirming God's presence in his life.

p. 14, ll. 9-14

Bill W. could not accept all the tenets of the Oxford Groups, but he was convinced of the need for these five things: (1) a personal moral inventory; (2) the confession of his personality defects; (3) restitution to the people he had harmed through his alcoholism; (4) continued helpfulness to others; and, most important, (5) the belief in and dependence upon a Higher Power.

After his awakening, Bill W. worked hard to help many other alcoholics in New York City. He felt that only an alcoholic could help an alcoholic; but, although he was staying sober himself, he didn't succeed in helping anyone else break the addiction to alcohol. He was probably jerking people off bar stools, talking to them in the gutters, finding alcoholics anywhere he could. But none of them responded to what he had to offer.

One day, while talking to another alcoholic in the hospital, he ran into Dr. Silkworth again. Their conversation might have been something like this:

"Doctor," Bill said, "I've been trying to give away what I've received, and nobody seems to want it."

The doctor told him, "Bill, you're probably trying to cram that great white flash you had down their throats. That doesn't work. If you try to cram anything down the throat of an alcoholic, he'll just puke it right back up every time. What you need to do is tell them what their problem is. Tell them what I told you. Explain to them the nature of the problem and the mental and physical components of their disease. Every alcoholic I know wants to know two things: (1) *Why can't I drink like I used to without getting drunk?* and (2) *Why can't I quit now that I want to quit?* If you can answer those two questions for them, you'll get their attention. And then you'll be able to tell them about a spiritual means of recovery. But don't give them the spirituality first because you'll turn them off every time."

The Fellowship Begins

By now it's the middle of 1935. We don't think it was an accident that right after Bill W. had his conversation with Dr. Silkworth, he contacted Dr. Bob in Akron. Bill had gone there to put together a business deal. There was a proxy fight going on over an Akron-based company, and if things worked out as Bill had hoped, he was going to end up becoming president of the company. But to Bill's distress, the deal fell through.

So picture this: Bill W. stood in the lobby of the Mayflower Hotel in Akron, counting his money, and realized he didn't even have enough to pay his hotel bill. He was feeling very sad, very depressed, very low. He happened to look through a door that led to the hotel bar. Like most bars, the lights were probably low; music was playing; the smoke was thick; and the people were laughing. Bill probably said to himself, "I'll go in and have a soda and maybe I'll feel better. I won't drink, but at least I'll be with people of my kind." But as he started to go through the door, he must have heard himself think, *You can't do that; if you go in there, you're going to get drunk.* Bill realized he needed some help if he was to stay sober.

Through a series of phone calls, Bill came in contact with Dr. Bob. Dr. Bob had repeatedly tried spiritual means to resolve his alcoholic dilemma, but had failed. To Bill's amazement, he learned that Dr. Bob had been going to the Oxford Groups for quite some time. He had been trying to apply their program in his life, but he was unable to do it as deeply as he needed to because he didn't understand what was wrong with him. He still thought the problem was a weak will, or a lack of moral character, or sin. At least, this was what nearly everyone had told him the problem was. But when Bill W. gave him Dr. Silkworth's description of the disease of alcoholism, he began to pursue the spiritual remedy for his illness with a willingness he never had before.

This might have been one of the first miracles of Alcoholics Anonymous. Picture this: an old, broken-down, manipulating New York City speculator sits down with a well-trained physician and tells the physician what's wrong with his body and mind—and the physician not only listens to him, but believes him! It seems to us that normally any doctor would have said, "Who the hell are you to tell me what's wrong with my mind and body?" But Bill W.'s message had such depth and interest that Dr. Bob found himself embracing it almost immediately.

Dr. Bob then began to apply the program in his life. He got drunk one more time, but then he sobered up, never to drink again until he died in 1950. This seemed to demonstrate that one alcoholic could help another in a way that no nonalcoholic could. This is one of the basic principles behind AA, and it's one of the main reasons we wrote this book. Because we're alcoholics ourselves, we know what it's like to be in your shoes, and we can understand and help you in a way other people can't.

So Bill W. and Dr. Bob set to work almost frantically to help alcoholics in the Akron City Hospital. Their very first case, a man named Bill D., was a desperate one, but he recovered immediately and became AA member number three. Bill W. and Dr. Bob told Bill D. three things: (1) They told him what his problem really was—something no one else had ever told him before. (2) They told him that the solution to his problem would be a vital spiritual experience. (3) And they told him about a practical program of action that they had both used to recover. Then they said to Bill D., "You can do this, too, if you want to."

A day or so later, Bill D. said to his wife, "Get my clothes out of the closet. I'm going home." He left the hospital, applied the program in his life, sobered up, and never drank again for the rest of his life.

So, in the summer of 1935 in Akron, Ohio, there were three people who knew three things: (1) what the problem was, (2) what the solution was, and (3) what the practical program for achieving that solution was.

Early Growth and Plans of AA

Bill W. stayed on in Akron for a while, and he and Dr. Bob kept working with the alcoholics in the Akron hospital. There were many failures, but there were occasional successes too. Also, a small number of people who had recovered had formed a group. This nameless bunch of drunks was really the first AA group, although they hadn't yet come up with the name Alcoholics Anonymous.

In the fall of 1935, Bill W. returned to New York, taking his knowledge of the problem, the solution, and the practical program of action with him. By 1937, a second small group had formed in New York. Also, some alcoholics, who had picked up the basic ideas behind AA in Akron or New York, were trying to form similar groups in other cities.

During that year, Bill W. went back to Akron to make a second attempt at taking over that same company—something he never did manage to do. While he was there he went to a meeting with Dr. Bob. They counted heads and found that there were nearly forty alcoholics who were staying sober in Akron and New York. They began to think, *Maybe we have something here that can work for lots of people. How can we get the message out to other alcoholics?*

They decided to call another meeting later that evening to try to answer this question. Eighteen people showed up, and they took a vote on what they should do. By a narrow margin, the group voted to do three things. Now, the first two were the kind of grandiose ideas you'd expect from a bunch of alcoholics who didn't have an extra dime among them. They wanted to build a chain of hospitals across the country to treat alcoholics. They thought they would then hire, train, and pay a group of missionaries to carry their message. Of course, neither of these ideas ever happened.

The third thing they decided to do was write a book.

The Writing of the Big Book

At this point, the AA program had come together pretty well. They had the idea of the problem, the solution, and the practical program of action. But all this was being passed on from one person to another entirely by word of mouth, and that worried some people a little bit.

You know how we alcoholics are: We start adding things to whatever we hear, and taking other things away according to how we want things to suit us at the time. The Akron group felt that if the message wasn't in written form, it would be hard to preserve accurately. They also felt that the book they'd write would be the first definitive book on alcoholism. Their hope was that it would be a big seller so they could make some money and build their hospitals and pay their missionaries.

At first, the people in the group decided that they wanted Bill W. to write this book. They said something like, "Bill, you're the guy who started this thing. You've been sober longer than the rest of us, and you know more about this recovery program than we do. We want you to write it in the same sequence we had to learn it in, and we want you to include the same information we had to learn." But they might have also told Bill, "We don't want it to be your book, though; it's got to be *our* book. As you write it, we want to see each chapter, and we'll change things around however we want. That way when we're through with it, it'll have the collective knowledge and experience of all of us rather than just one person's." Bill agreed, and the work began.

It took two years to write the book, which was titled *Alcoholics Anonymous*. By the time it was finished, in 1939, membership in the groups had reached about one hundred men and women. The society, which had been nameless until now, also began to be called Alcoholics Anonymous from the title of its book.

The book *Alcoholics Anonymous*, which many of us now just call the Big Book, after a shaky start, turned out to be an even bigger success than any of the early AA people had hoped. It has sold millions of copies, been reprinted dozens of times, and been translated into many different languages.

There is something else particularly interesting about the book: It has remained largely unchanged since its first edition in 1939. The first portion of the Big Book, describing the AA program for recovery in detail, has been left untouched for over fifty years.* There is a very good reason for this: The program it describes works, and has been working for millions of people throughout the world, year after year.

Now you know something about how the organization Alcoholics Anonymous and the book by the same name came to be. In the chapters to come we'll show you how the Big Book presents a clear, step-by-step sequence for solving your own alcohol or other addiction problem. We will also show you how and why following that whole sequence is so important.

---

* Because *Alcoholics Anonymous* was published in 1939 when the male gender pronoun was considered to be inclusive of women, some language in the Big Book appears to exclude women. This was not consciously intended. The suggestions and principles in the Big Book apply to *all* alcoholics. Most women coming to AA and other Twelve Step programs have read past these archaic conventions and found the truth that is there.

—EDITOR

CHAPTER TWO

Using the Big Book Correctly

Following the Big Book's Program of Action

When the Big Book was first published in 1939, the people in the Alcoholics Anonymous fellowship practiced and worked the recovery program in the book. What the book said and what AA members did were the same.

Over the past fifty-some years, the Big Book has changed very little, and its most important sections have remained exactly the same. But the AA fellowship and the other Twelve Step fellowships that have followed have changed a great deal. We have brought in so many different things, adding to the program and watering it down, that sometimes it hardly resembles the Twelve Step program in the Big Book at all. We think this is a big mistake.

We have heard that at some meetings today, people are told, "Just go to meetings for ninety days and don't drink, and you'll be okay." But this isn't what the Big Book says. You can look through it from cover to cover, and you won't find that message anywhere.

In the fellowship of AA and other Twelve Step support groups, people find a lot of strength through sharing with one another and supporting each other. We think this is extremely valuable. But some years back, a few people found that they could stay sober on fellowship only, without actually working the Twelve Step program. So they began to water the program down a little bit, and then a little bit more, one inch at a time. Eventually, things got watered down so much that people in the fellowship began saying all kinds of things that aren't in the Big Book at all.

For instance, we've heard a lot of people say, "You can apply the program cafeteria style. Take what you want, leave what you want, and everything will be okay." But we don't believe this is true. The program is a single, unified whole, not a collection of tidbits of advice. There is nothing in the Big Book that says, "Treat the Twelve Step program like a smorgasbord."

Some of what gets said in meetings that's not part of the AA recovery program is harmless. But some things can do real damage, and some can be deadly. We have heard something in meetings that has killed a lot of people, and that almost killed one of us. It goes like this: "If you come to meetings long enough, you'll soak up all the important things by osmosis, and everything will be great." We disagree strongly with this. We don't think the Twelve Step program works by osmosis. You have to apply it in your own life, and that takes effort.

Today things have been watered down and changed around so much that you can go to some AA meetings and, if someone didn't read the AA preamble to the meeting, you'd have no idea what kind of meeting you were actually attending. We find this to be true in meetings throughout the country—not all of them, of course, but some. Sometimes in AA meetings people talk about everything *except* recovering from the disease of alcoholism and the application of the Twelve Steps in their lives.

We don't doubt that the people who bring these ideas to the fellowship mean well. But we need to point out that the Big Book doesn't deal with fellowship at all. It deals with the program of recovery as used by the first one hundred people in AA. *The fellowship came out of the program, not the other way around.*

The Effectiveness of the Big Book

If you look at the top of page xx in the Big Book, you'll see   p. xx, ll. 1-9
just how effective the book was when the fellowship's
recovery program and the recovery program described in
the book were the same. Page xx explains that AA grew by
leaps and bounds because many people recovered through
it and many families were reunited because of it. Half of all
the alcoholics who came to AA and seriously and sincerely
tried to recover got sober immediately and stayed that way.
Another 25 percent sobered up a little more slowly.

So in the beginning, when the fellowship program and
the program in the Big Book were the same, it is estimated
that 75 percent of the people who used the Twelve Step
program and really tried to recover from the disease of
alcoholism actually did. We wonder what the percentage is
today. We doubt very seriously if it's 50 percent, let alone 75
percent.

We don't think drunks today are much different than
they were in 1939, and certainly alcohol isn't any different
today than in 1939. The Big Book hasn't changed much,
either, since the days when probably 75 percent of all the
people who read it and followed its Twelve Step program
recovered from the disease of alcoholism. The only thing
that has really changed is the fellowship itself.

We believe that this is the big problem in many AA
meetings today. It's a serious problem, too, because far
fewer people are recovering from their illness. We have
written this book in part to explain how and why we think
the fellowship has gotten into trouble—but mostly we want
to point the way back to the Big Book. We hope to show you
how the program it offers can help you recover from your
addiction to alcohol (and, we believe, to other drugs and
addictive behaviors as well), and to help you use that
program most effectively.

Old-Timers and Newcomers

Part of the problem, as we see it, has to do with the differences between some of the newer people in the fellowship and the old-timers who have been in it for years and years. Of course, new people are always joining the fellowship, and we're glad they keep joining. Many of them, though, use a language and terms that a lot of old-timers aren't used to. That is nobody's fault—but what happens is that some old-timers begin saying, "We don't identify with these people. We're tired of hearing what they have to say, so we're just going to stay home." The problem is that when the old-timers stay home, they abdicate their responsibility to carry their message to other alcoholics, as explained in Step Twelve. The meetings then get turned over to the new people, who are the sickest of the sick.

Instead of staying home, the old-timers need to keep coming to meetings and say to newcomers, "Look, we know that everything you learned is important to you, and we're not telling you it's wrong, but here's what we talk about in AA." Then the old-timers need to talk about the Twelve Steps and how the program works. They need to train newcomers in the basic principles and language of AA, and keep the fellowship meetings on track. When a meeting starts to wander away from the Twelve Steps and the program, it's the old-timers' job to bring it back.

There are people in AA today—including some who have been in the fellowship for months or years—who never actually read all of the Big Book, or even a large part of it. We think this is a mistake. For most alcoholics, reading the Big Book is an essential part of recovery; it's not just a supplement to AA meetings. *If you truly wish to recover from the disease of alcoholism, we urge you to actually read the Big Book from beginning to end. In fact, we urge you to read it right away. If you haven't read any of the Big Book yet, please put down our book now and start in on the Big Book immediately.*

Now you know how the Big Book came about and how important we think it is to your recovery. Next we'll take a close look at the central problem we alcoholics all share. The Big Book explains this problem clearly and in great detail. Then we'll examine the practical, step-by-step solutions the Big Book gives us to overcome this problem, and how you can put those solutions to work in your own life.

CHAPTER THREE

Understanding the Problem

The very first thing you have to do to solve a problem is find out what that problem is. This sounds simple, but it often isn't. In order to find a real, lasting solution, you have to understand the problem thoroughly and know exactly what it is. Until you have this information, you can't solve your problem. If your roof is leaking, you can't begin to fix it until you find the hole.

Usually when you have a problem, you can go to a professional—a doctor, a dentist, a car mechanic—and that person can find out what your problem is and tell you. But alcoholism and other drug addictions are the only diseases in which the patient has to make his or her own diagnosis. It won't do any good to have a doctor tell you, "You're powerless over alcohol [or cocaine, marijuana, etcetera]." You must make this diagnosis yourself.

This is very hard to do because alcoholism and other drug addictions are diseases that tell the patient, "You haven't got it; you're fine." That is how you can tell who has the disease: If someone swears, "I haven't got it," it's pretty certain the person does.

The Nature of the Problem

What exactly is the problem? The Big Book tells us, without pulling any punches, in Step One of the Twelve Steps: *The problem is that we're powerless over alcohol and our lives have become unmanageable.* Understanding and accepting this will be the first step in your recovery.

It all boils down to that one word: *powerless*. Once we really see this and accept it, then we can understand that there's a solution. Until we fully understand this, however, we're still lost.

Once we do know that the problem is powerlessness, the solution has to be power. It's that simple. Power is the cure for powerlessness. Now we have both the diagnosis—powerlessness—and the prescription—power.

Since we can't do anything about the physical part of the illness of alcoholism, our solution must be to find a power that can work in a non-physical way, in our mind. Step Two of the Twelve Step program says that we "came to believe that a Power greater than ourselves could restore us to sanity." That is the power we're talking about. We believe that this is the foundation of the whole Alcoholics Anonymous program.

Now, if you're powerless and the solution to your problem is power, then what you need to do is find that power. Steps Three through Twelve enable us to find a Higher Power, a Power greater than ourselves. *The main purpose of the Big Book is to enable you to find a Power greater than yourself that will solve your problem.*

The Three Stages of Recovery

What the Big Book looks at, then, are three things: (1) powerlessness, (2) power, and (3) finding that power. These will be the three stages of your recovery. They are the same things Bill W., Dr. Bob, Bill D., and every one of those first one hundred people had to know to recover from their illness.

So, the three basic questions of the Big Book, and of any recovery program, are these:

1. What is the problem?
2. What is the solution?
3. What is the program of action necessary for me to find and to use or implement that solution?

The Big Book is a basic textbook for answering all three of these questions. As you go through the Big Book with us, you'll see that it's written in standard textbook form, proceeding logically, step by step and chapter by chapter. *It was written to be used as the textbook for your recovery.* You can use it just like you'd use any other textbook. "The Doctor's Opinion" and Chapter 1 explain the exact nature of the problem (Step One). Chapters 2, 3, and 4 provide the solution (Step Two). The planned program of action, your recovery plan, is explained Step by Step in Chapters 5, 6, and 7 (Steps Three through Twelve). Followed this way, *Alcoholics Anonymous* has become the basic text for recovery for millions of people.

Using the Big Book as a Textbook for Your Recovery

When we think of a textbook, we think of a tool that is used to transfer knowledge from the mind of one human being to another. We all know that in order to use a textbook properly, you have to read and study it. You have to do some work to understand the material and absorb the knowledge that the book provides. Once that transfer of knowledge has been made, however, you know the same things the writer of the book knew when it was written.

A good textbook is deliberately written in a particular sequence. Most textbooks assume that the reader knows very little about the subject, so they start out at the beginning on a very simple level, with the most basic principles. As the reader's knowledge increases with each chapter, the material presented normally starts to become more difficult.

For example, imagine a basic mathematics textbook, one for people who can't do much more than count. The book would begin with addition and subtraction, then work up to multiplication, division, fractions, and so on, eventually building up to things such as algebra.

Let's say we meet a person who knows nothing about math, and he asks us for a book that will help him learn about the subject. Suppose we hand this person a textbook and say, "Here. Why don't you start with Chapter 5 and work on some of the algebra problems?" So he looks at Chapter 5, but of course he doesn't know anything about addition or subtraction, let alone algebra. The symbols look like hen scratchings to him. He'll be completely lost, and chances are that he'll close the book, put it down, and never pick it up again.

But if we say instead, "Here's a mathematics textbook. Take a look at Chapter 1, which deals with addition and subtraction. If you read it and study it and ask questions when you need to, by the time you're done with Chapter 1, you'll know how to add and subtract." So the person reads Chapter 1 and, to nobody's surprise, he learns addition and subtraction. Next we say, "Now why don't you read Chapter 2, and you'll learn how to multiply and divide." So he does that, and pretty soon he's ready for Chapter 3. Gradually, we lead him through the textbook until eventually he's ready to learn algebra in Chapter 5.

We believe one of the greatest mistakes being made today among AA groups, and other fellowships using the Big Book, is that they don't help people to start from the beginning. When newcomers walk in the door, they're often told, "Get a copy of *Alcoholics Anonymous,* go to Chapter 5, do what the author says, and you'll be all right." So the newcomer turns straight to Chapter 5, and the first thing she reads are the Twelve Steps and about how they work. But to her they may look like algebra problems because she's just not ready for them yet. The person hasn't been prepared for them at all.

In fact, the newcomer probably doesn't even understand what each of the Steps means. Take Step One, for instance. It says:

> We admitted we were powerless over alcohol—
> that our lives had become unmanageable.

She may read this and say, "Man, don't tell me I'm powerless. I'm not powerless over anything." She doesn't know what the Big Book means by this statement because she hasn't read any of the earlier chapters or the introductory sections.

But maybe, without any preparation, she makes it through Step One, accepts it, and is ready to keep going. Next, she reads Step Two, which says, "Came to believe that a Power greater than ourselves could restore us to sanity." Here she may stop and say, "Hell, I'm not crazy! I may do stupid things while I'm drinking, but when I'm sober, I'm as sane as the next person." She doesn't understand what the Big Book is talking about at all.

Think about it for a moment. If you're not powerless and you're not nuts, then you don't need to decide to turn your will and your life over to the care of some Power you don't understand. And if you *think* you're not powerless, even though the truth is that you are, then you're certainly not about to turn your will and your life over to anyone.

This is why starting out cold with Chapter 5 and the Twelve Steps, as many people and fellowship groups do, sometimes does more harm than good. Sometimes starting out with Chapter 5 only turns people away from AA, from the Twelve Steps, and from recovery.

We believe that "The Doctor's Opinion" (pages xxiii-xxx) and Chapters 1 through 4 (pages 1-57) are deliberately designed to prepare you for Chapter 5. *If we can convince you of nothing else in this chapter, we hope we'll get you to understand how important these chapters in the Big Book are in preparing you to accept and begin working the Steps presented in Chapter 5.* These portions of the Big Book teach you how to add, subtract, multiply, and divide. They prepare you for the algebra problems you'll get once you reach Chapter 5.

A Recipe for Recovery

There is another way of looking at the Big Book, and that's as a recipe book. When you think about it, a recipe book is a kind of textbook. It shows you step by step how to make certain dishes. It works the same way as a math textbook, except that instead of math problems, you have directions for cooking different foods. If you follow a recipe the way the book says, you'll get the dish you're trying to make, and it will taste the way it's supposed to. If you follow the same steps each time, the dish will turn out the same way and taste the same every time.

Let's say you've just baked a delicious strawberry cake, and you've given each of us a big piece. We take a few bites, and both of us agree that everything about the cake is just right: the taste, the texture, the moisture content, the sweetness—all just perfect. So we say to you, "This is terrific cake. Can we get the recipe?" Being an obliging person, you write out the directions for us, telling us how to make a cake exactly like the one we've been eating. You tell us the quantity of the ingredients to use, the sequence in which to mix them, what temperature to bake the cake at, and how long to bake it. If we follow your directions precisely, our cake will turn out exactly like your cake.

But suppose instead of following your recipe, our keen intellectual minds start saying, *No, it really shouldn't have three eggs; it should have six. Instead of two cups of sugar, we'll put in five. And instead of baking it for forty minutes at 375 degrees, we'll bake it for an hour and a half at 550.* When that thing comes out of the oven, it'll be some sort of cake. But how closely is it going to resemble the strawberry cake you make? More likely, it'll resemble a concrete block or a great big piece of burnt toast. Since our whole point was to make a cake just like the one you did, we've gotten in the way of our own intentions by tinkering with the recipe.

We have a clear recipe for recovery in the book *Alcoholics Anonymous.* It tells us exactly what to do every step of the way. The book shows us precisely how the first one hundred or so people recovered from the same disease you have. If you follow their recipe and do the same things they did, then we believe you'll end up just where they did: freed from your addiction to alcohol and other drugs. If you start tinkering with the recipe, though, as some people and groups have been doing, you may end up somewhere very different.

What Makes the Big Book Special

A couple of other things strike us about the Big Book being a step-by-step guidebook for recovery. First, most textbooks get updated from time to time, as people make new discoveries and expand their knowledge on the subject. Recipe books get updated, too, as cooks come up with new recipes and tastier or easier-to-cook variations. The Big Book has been updated a couple of times too—once in 1955, and again in 1976. The section of personal stories in the back has been added to, subtracted from, and changed around a little. *But the first 164 pages and the introductory material, which together form the recovery program, have been left untouched.* Why? Because since 1939, when the book was first published, nobody has been able to improve on the recovery program described in the first edition. In all the fifty-some years that have passed since the Big Book's first edition, no one has come up with a better recipe. The Twelve Step program works as well now as it did in 1939.

Here is something else we think is important: The Big Book is the work of over one hundred people. Sure, Bill W. did the writing, but over one hundred people, all of them recovering alcoholics, helped determine what he wrote. They told Bill W. what to write—and once he'd written it, they told him how to change it. By the time the book was finished, it was the collective work of dozens of different people.

Most every book we read today is written by one person or, at most, two or three. If we read a book and don't agree with what the author says, we can feel free to think, *Who is he to think he knows more than I do?* But it's much harder to do this with the Big Book, because then we'd be arguing not with just one person, but with over one hundred. And of these hundred-plus people, every one of them has recovered from the same disease you have and we have. To us, that means these folks are worth listening to.

In the next two chapters we'll listen to Dr. Silkworth and what he has to teach us. Then we'll listen to Bill W.'s story and discover how we can benefit from his experience and follow in his footsteps.

CHAPTER FOUR

The Twofold Disease Of Alcoholism

"The Doctor's Opinion" (pages xxiii-xxx) is the foundation of the whole book *Alcoholics Anonymous* and of the entire AA fellowship. To non-alcoholics and non-addicts, this section may simply seem to be a helpful introductory note, but without it, the entire book doesn't make sense. In this chapter of our own book we want to examine closely and carefully what Dr. William D. Silkworth wrote. We hope you'll come to see just how important his words and conclusions will be to your own recovery.

Dr. Silkworth was the first physician to fully understand and put into words what an alcoholic's problem is. He was the first to see the problem fully, clearly, and correctly. This was his main contribution to medicine and to AA.

Misunderstandings About Alcoholism

It sounds strange, but the fact is that sixty-some years ago, no one really understood alcoholism. By then cars, airplanes, radios, and telephones were commonplace, but people were still in the dark about alcoholism. Even though alcohol and alcoholics had been around for thousands of years, nobody really knew what the problem was with alcoholics.

From the time people first started drinking alcohol, some of them had problems with it. The majority of people, those who didn't drink, or those who did but didn't have any problem with it, were puzzled by alcoholics. It was easy to see that the alcoholics had a problem, but it wasn't clear what the problem was. So the non-alcoholics did their best to figure out what was wrong with the alcoholics. They came up with all kinds of guesses and theories, most of them pretty far off the mark.

Down through history, it's always been this way: the non-alcoholics have been trying to figure out the alcoholics. Non-alcoholics would look at an alcoholic and say, "What's wrong with this person? He must be weak, or sinful, or crazy." The non-alcoholics had a hard time even figuring out what alcoholics felt or went through, let alone what their problem might be. As for the alcoholics, they didn't care very much what their problem was or what non-alcoholics thought; they just kept on drinking.

This has been going on for centuries. If you look in the Bible, you'll find Solomon spent some time describing alcoholics in Prov. 23:29-35. He referred to them as "they who tarry long over the wine," and he described them as people who babble and "utter perverse things," who have red eyes and "wounds without cause," who end up sleeping anywhere, from right in the sea to on top of a mast, and who, when they wake up miserable from their binge on alcohol, "will seek" it yet again. This description certainly fits alcoholics of our time as well as Solomon's. So Solomon clearly observed and described the disease of alcoholism—though he didn't understand the problem.

Dr. Benjamin Rush, back in 1784, was one of the first physicians to say about alcoholism, "I believe that this is a disease process." That's an exact quote. He also said, "I believe the answer is total abstinence." Not *an* answer—*the* answer. You might have heard of Dr. Rush before; he was one of the signers of the Declaration of Independence. Unfortunately, people didn't pay much attention to Dr. Rush's views on alcoholism; at that time, it was still being regarded as a moral issue, and as a sin.

Dr. Silkworth's Breakthrough

It wasn't until around one hundred and fifty years later that someone really understood the problem, and that someone was Dr. Silkworth. Dr. Silkworth began working with alcoholics in 1930. He worked closely with them, looking for clues and patterns in the ways they lived and acted. He studied his patients carefully, looking for any traits they might share, and he came up with something awfully interesting. He discovered that alcoholics had some driving self-destructive force in them.

His breakthrough came when he was able to divide this force into two separate drives: a physical craving, and an obsession in the mind. He wrote, "I believe part of this is in their body and part of it in their mind."

If we look at lines 10-21 on page xxiv of the Big Book, we learn that Dr. Silkworth confirmed that both the body and mind of the alcoholic are abnormal. This is the first time in medical history where there is any direct reference to the fact that the body is affected as well as the mind. Up until this point, what people had thought and said about alcoholism and alcoholics had to do entirely with the mind. Alcoholics were thought to be sinful, corrupt, weak-willed, or lacking in moral character. p. xxiv, ll. 10-21

But as it says on page xxiv, Dr. Silkworth felt that alcoholism was a form of allergy. Alcoholics are people who have an allergic reaction to alcohol. The hundred or so alcoholics—who had solved their drinking problems and who had overseen the writing of the Big Book—agreed that Dr. Silkworth's explanation made sense and that it explained many things that couldn't otherwise be explained. p. xxiv, ll. 22-27

Alcoholism as an Allergy

That word Dr. Silkworth used—*allergy*—probably gives some people more trouble than any other word in the Big Book, so we want to consider it carefully. It is important that we understand exactly what Dr. Silkworth meant by an allergy.

Before the two of us came to AA or read the Big Book, we thought we knew what the word *allergy* meant. We knew that if you were allergic to something, and you ate or drank or breathed some of it, you'd have a physical reaction. If you're allergic to strawberries and you eat some strawberry cake, you'll break out in a rash. If you're allergic to ragweed and you breathe in some ragweed pollen, your eyes will itch and you'll start to sneeze.

When the two of us first came to AA, we were told, "Fellows, you're allergic to alcohol and you'll never be able to safely drink it again." Well, the first thing we thought was, *How can we be allergic to alcohol? We've been drinking a quart a day. We don't get rashes from it, and we don't start sneezing because of it. How can you drink that much of something you're allergic to?* We thought that if you're allergic to something, it meant you had to have a visible physical reaction to it, like sneezing or hives. But if you look in a dictionary, you'll see that one of the definitions of an allergy is an abnormal reaction to a food, beverage, or other substance—not necessarily sneezing or itching or vomiting, but *any* abnormal reaction.

Now, the funny thing about having an abnormal reaction is that you can't tell whether something is abnormal or not until you know what normal is. When we first got into AA and were told that we were allergic to alcohol, we had to admit that we didn't know what normal was. We knew what we felt and how we acted when we took a drink, but we didn't know if that was normal; we didn't know if other people felt and acted the same way. The only thing we knew about alcohol was the way we drank it and the way those who drank with us drank it. (You see, if people didn't drink like we did, we didn't drink with them.)

Eventually, we realized that to find out what was normal, we'd have to talk to people who weren't affected by alcohol like we were—the so-called social drinkers. We asked some of these people, "How do you feel whenever you take a drink?" And they'd answer something like this: "Well, I get home from work feeling tired, tense, and wrought up. I have a drink or two before dinner and, in a little while, I get a comfortable, relaxing feeling. Then I have dinner, and usually I don't drink any more that night."

At first we were a little shocked by this because that's not the way we felt at all when we drank alcohol. When either of us would take a drink, we'd begin to respond instantly. As the alcohol would pass over our lips, they'd begin to tingle. It would cross our teeth, and they'd kind of chatter up and down. When it hit our tongues, we could feel them expand and swell. Then it would reach our cheeks, and they'd flutter in and out a little. We could feel it passing up through our sinus cavities and into our foreheads, and we'd get a feeling in our foreheads that was absolutely, indescribably wonderful. And we wouldn't even have swallowed it yet—the first sip would still be in our mouths!

Once we did swallow, great things would begin to happen. Our chests would seem to grow and expand. Then the alcohol would hit our stomachs and explode like a bomb. We'd immediately feel it racing through our arms. When it reached our hands and fingers, they'd begin to tingle and vibrate. The alcohol would race through our legs, and we'd feel like we were getting taller. Then it would hit our feet and toes, and we'd experience an intense, exciting get-up-and-go-somewhere-and-do-something feeling.

Now that's awfully different from the warm, relaxing feeling most people get when they drink.

Social Drinking and the Myth of Willpower

When we talked to some of the normal, average social drinkers, we also asked them how they felt when they had several drinks in a row. They told us that they would get a slightly tipsy, out-of-control, nauseous feeling. "We don't like that nauseous feeling," they said to us, "so two or three drinks are all we have, and all we want."

After we'd talked to enough people and heard them say the same thing, we realized that this is the normal reaction to alcohol. It is a sedative drug, so it's supposed to make you slightly tipsy and a little out of control. Since alcohol is a destroyer of human tissue, the body is supposed to react to too much of it with nausea. When you put too much of it into the body, the body will vomit it back up to get rid of it.

This answered a huge question for us. We had always thought that social drinkers used willpower to stop after only one or two drinks. In fact, that's one of the things they'd often say to us: "All you have to do is use willpower, like I do." But they don't *have* to use willpower at all because one to three drinks are all they want or need. They get all they want to drink every time they drink, so it's easy for them to stop.

For years we'd look at those normal social drinkers and wonder about them. They would have two drinks, and when somebody offered them a third, they'd say, "Oh, no, I feel this one already," or "No, I'm getting sleepy," or "No, it'll make me sick." We never understood how people could say these sorts of things because that's not how alcohol made us feel.

When we would drink alcohol, we'd never feel slightly tipsy or out of control or nauseous. We would feel *in* control. Instead of reacting with nausea, our bodies would say, "Drink some more alcohol." Our bodies would produce an acute physical craving—one so strong that we couldn't imagine how we'd be able to stop drinking. We would plan on having only two drinks, but once either of us had put those two into his system, the physical craving would develop. Then the body would take over, and the mind would no longer be in control. We'd have a third drink, and a fourth, and we'd keep drinking, and soon we'd be in all kinds of trouble.

That is an abnormal reaction to alcohol.

Please understand that "abnormal" doesn't mean "bad" or "weak" or "wrong"—it's just different from what most people experience. The only difference between normal and abnormal is that normal is what most people do. It so happens that about one person in ten reacts in much the same way we do when he or she takes a drink. Those people have an allergic reaction to alcohol, just like we do. If you react to alcohol in pretty much the same way, you've got the allergy too.

After talking to people, both of us realized that our reaction to alcohol was abnormal, and we began to understand why neither of us could drink without getting drunk. We also began to see how our drinking must have looked to normal people. *We had to accept that when it comes to alcohol, we are different from most people.* When normal people feel the effect of alcohol, they're ready and able to stop drinking. But when alcoholics feel the effect of alcohol, they want to keep on drinking. Now some may be able to white-knuckle it and limit their intake a few times. But inevitably they'll come to a point where they can't stop. Eventually, the physical craving will be impossible for their minds to control. Not *very difficult*—literally *impossible.* In lines 1-3 of page xxviii in "The Doctor's Opinion," Dr. Silkworth says that this physical craving is simply beyond all mental control. p. xxviii, ll. 1-3

We heard someone say once that the difference between social drinkers and alcoholics is that social drinkers go to a party to socialize and may have a drink or two. Alcoholics go to a party to drink and might incidentally socialize as long as they are there.

Normal people do not crave alcohol. We alcoholics do.

The Physical Craving Caused by Alcohol

We believe that, in AA, people sometimes don't talk enough about the physical part of the illness of alcoholism. Part of our problem as alcoholics is in our mind, but another part is in our body.

Most health problems are physical; some are mental or emotional. But alcoholism is an unusual illness because it affects both the body and the mind. The mental part of the disease is an obsession with alcohol; the physical part is an intense craving for alcohol. The two aspects of the illness are quite different, as we'll soon see, but they work closely together.

The physical craving is part of our allergy to alcohol. It's a reaction to having alcohol in our system. Now, notice that the physical craving begins *after we drink, not before.* Alcohol in our body makes us crave more alcohol.

The initial impulse to take that first drink *isn't* physical. We might have a psychological compulsion or an obsession to drink, but we cannot experience a *physical* craving unless we put alcohol into our body. That's how the allergy works.

In the Big Book, the word "craving" always refers to the body—to the *physical* craving that occurs only *after* you've taken a drink. That's how we'll use the word in this book too. As for the desires of the mind, we'll use other words.

So now we know that part of our problem as alcoholics is purely physical. Once we start drinking, we eventually won't be able to get ourselves to stop. It's that simple, and it's a fact. We can't stop. If you're an alcoholic and you tell yourself that you *can* take a drink and then stop, you're in trouble.

The Answer Is Abstinence

p. xxviii, ll. 30-31

p. xxviii, ll. 13-23

The one way to stay out of trouble is to not take that first drink. Dr. Silkworth says this quite plainly, on lines 30-31 of page xxviii, in "The Doctor's Opinion." He states clearly that the only relief from alcoholism comes from total abstinence. There are no compromises; there is no middle ground.

On this same page, on lines 13 through 23, Dr. Silkworth classifies the different types of alcoholics. There is the manic-depressive type, the unstable type, the friendly type—all sorts of different types. Some alcoholics cry in their beer; others get up on the table and start hooting and hollering. Some get into fights; others put the make on each other. But there's one thing every one of us alcoholics, regardless of our personality, has in common: at some point, once we start drinking, we'll go looking for another drink, and another, and on and on until we're drunk and sick and in trouble.

Some of us are born alcoholics. Other people drink themselves into alcoholism. For years, some people can drink with relative safety, but then they seem to cross a line somewhere and start getting into uncontrolled drinking. But it really doesn't make any difference how we came by our allergy to alcohol, because the end result is the same. It doesn't matter how long it takes us to get drunk, either. Both of us know from the years when we used to drink that if we took a drink at five minutes after ten, by noon we'd be in jail somewhere. Other alcoholics go at a much slower pace. Some might take a drink or two today, three or four tomorrow, five or six the next day—it might take them a week to end up in jail or in some other kind of trouble. But it doesn't make any difference how long it takes because *what triggers it all is that first drink they take.*

If you're an alcoholic, so long as you try to figure out a way to drink without getting drunk, or a way to stop after one or two drinks, you've got a problem. You're going to end up drunk. As long as you think that you can drink, that some day you'll be able to drink like most people, you'll keep drinking, getting drunk, and getting into trouble. This is the truth that Bill W., Dr. Bob, Bill D., and every one of those first one hundred people in AA had to face. They each had to realize for themselves that they were different, that they'd never be able to drink like most other people. They understood that they could no longer safely take a drink—not one. Other drug addicts and people with other addictive behaviors have been finding the same thing. There appears to be something in their makeup—possibly their brain chemistry—that leaves them prone to the same kind of craving once they return to their mood-altering drug or behavior—no matter how long they've been abstinent.

Realizing this for yourself is the first step in your own recovery. In fact, Step One of the Twelve Steps says:

> We admitted we were powerless over alcohol—
> that our lives had become unmanageable.

The human mind is a funny thing. It will go on thinking in the same direction indefinitely—until you shut the door on that train of thought. The mind will start thinking in a different direction only when information comes along to shut that door for good.

This is what made Dr. Silkworth's discovery so important. He was able to tell alcoholics exactly what they had to do—quit drinking completely—and why—because they were allergic to alcohol.

The instant alcoholics realize what's really wrong with their bodies—that they've got an allergy and they'll never be able to get rid of it—then their thinking changes. Dr. Silkworth's information closes the door and shuts off the possibility of further drinking.

Only when you admit to yourself that you can never take another drink will you be able to deal with your illness and stop drinking for good. *All successful alcohol and other drug treatment programs are based on this one idea: Alcoholics or addicts will never be able to drink or use other drugs safely for as long as they live.*

CHAPTER FIVE

The Nature of Obsession

Today the medical profession has produced a great deal of evidence to confirm Dr. Silkworth's conclusions about alcoholism. There have been many medical studies that show that an alcoholic's body doesn't react to alcohol in the same way as a non-alcoholic's body does. When non-alcoholics drink, the alcohol gets broken down in their bodies in several stages: into water, sugar, and carbon dioxide. But there's been a lot of evidence that the alcohol doesn't get broken down in quite the same way in an alcoholic's body. Because of this, instead of getting tipsy, alcoholics crave more alcohol. The more they drink, the worse the craving gets. Drinking doesn't make the craving go away or even make it more bearable—in fact, it makes it stronger. It's like scratching a rash until it bleeds.

That is why when nearly everyone else is ready to go home, the alcoholic is just getting wound up and ready to continue partying. The physical craving is stronger after the twentieth drink than it was after the third. We never get all we want once we start drinking. *It's literally impossible to fill that craving.*

Here is something else the medical profession has turned up as evidence over the past few decades: Alcoholism is a progressive disease. That means the longer you have it, the worse it gets, even if you don't go anywhere near alcohol.

Neither of us has had a drink in over twenty years. But if we were to take a drink tomorrow, we wouldn't be in the same sorry condition we were in twenty-some years ago—

we'd be in *far worse* shape. The craving would be stronger, and our drinking would be much worse now than it was then.

Whenever we meet someone who had been sober for a while but who slipped and got drunk, we ask the person, "Was it any better this time?" And *invariably* the answer is that it was twice as bad as it was when the person was drinking before. The craving is worse, the drinking is worse, and the trouble that results is worse.

The Mental Aspect of Alcoholism

We have spent a lot of time discussing an alcoholic's physical craving that results from drinking alcohol because we feel strongly that the information is central to your recovery. But the whole question of what happens after we start drinking wouldn't matter if we didn't take that first drink.

So why *do* we take that first drink?

Remember, the physical craving doesn't begin until *after* there's already alcohol in your system. This means that whatever it is that makes you take that first drink must be entirely in your mind. It also means that *all of your recovery will also take place in your mind.*

p. xxvi,
ll. 30-31

On page xxvi, lines 30-31 (the beginning of the last paragraph on the page), Dr. Silkworth explains that people take that first drink because they like the effect alcohol produces in them. Many alcoholics get offended when they first read this. They say, "Oh, no, that isn't the reason I drink. I drink because I love the taste." Now, both of us love the taste of cold beer, and we also love the taste of cold mountain spring water. But neither one of us ever sat down and drank a case of mountain spring water. Alcohol does something to us that spring water doesn't.

p. xxvi,
ll. 34-35–
p. xxvii,
ll. 1-3

In this same paragraph, Dr. Silkworth describes how alcoholics often feel. They go around feeling *restless, irritable, and discontented* when they're sober. So their minds look for a way to feel happier and more content. They remember the pleasant way they felt the last time they had a few drinks—at least at first, before the awful craving kicked in. Eventually, these memories become strong enough, and they succumb and take the first couple of drinks. That sets off the intense physical craving, and they go on a drinking spree. They come out of that spree remorseful and start singing the alcoholic's national anthem—"I will never do that again." But then they go around in the same vicious circle again and again.

Dr. Silkworth says that this will keep happening over and over *until the alcoholic experiences a complete psychic change.* This psychic change enables the alcoholic to break the cycle.

p. xxvii,
ll. 7-9

If you're an alcoholic, somewhere in this cycle you'll get the idea in your head that taking a drink will provide relief and make you feel better. And the more you look at this idea, the more all other ideas get pushed out of your head. At this point, you can't remember the trouble you got into when you got drunk three weeks ago. Your mind triggers you to drink, so you take a drink, which triggers the craving in your body. The more you crave, the more you drink—and the more you drink, the more you crave.

Now let's jump ahead to the next time you become restless, irritable, and discontented. You'll remember what you did last time, which was take a drink. You'll also remember that taking a drink or two made you feel a little better—at first, anyway. You can't stop thinking about drinking as a way to make yourself feel better. This is called an *obsession*—an idea that overshadows and overcomes all other ideas. The alcoholic's obsession is the idea of taking a drink.

The fact is that you have to first think about drinking before you can actually take a drink. All action is born in thought—that's how an obsession works.

The Problem Reviewed

So, if you have an obsession with drinking, you can't keep from drinking because of your mind—but you can't drink safely because of the allergy in your body. Your mind makes you start drinking, and then your body won't let you stop. So your mind is slowly destroying your body, and your body is also being destructive to your mind.

If you can't drink because of your body, but you can't quit drinking because of your mind, then you are powerless over alcohol. Seeing this and realizing its truth is your first step in your recovery. It means you understand the problem.

The alcoholics who recover are the ones who clearly see this problem. Until you understand the problem, you're a victim of it; once you do understand it, you can recover from the disease of alcoholism. You won't be cured of your alcoholism—that's impossible. But you will recover from your hopeless condition of the mind and the body.

The problem isn't a weak will, or a lack of moral character, or the inability to resist the temptation of sin. The problem is a twofold disease: a physical allergy that ensures that once you start drinking you can't stop, and an obsession of the mind that ensures that you will, without recovery, always go back to drinking. Until you understand this problem clearly, your life will remain unmanageable.

All Obsessions Are Similar

We have been talking about an obsession with alcohol, but there are many different kinds of obsessions, and many people have them. Remember, an obsession is any idea that overcomes all other ideas, and it is so strong that it can make you believe things that aren't true. Some people are obsessed with eating certain foods. When some people with a food obsession eat a piece of chocolate candy, it can trigger a reaction in their bodies, in the same kind of way alcohol triggers an allergy in alcoholics. Once compulsive overeaters start eating, they can't stop, and they go on a binge, just like alcoholics do with alcohol. Then they emerge from the binge remorseful, with a firm resolution not to do it again—also just like alcoholics. Not surprisingly, pretty soon they start running around feeling restless, irritable, and discontented.

They want to start feeling better, and they begin to remember that initial pleasant feeling they get when they eat candy or whatever their favorite binge food is. The next thing you know, their minds have convinced them that they can safely eat it. So they eat some, which triggers their physical craving, and they just can't stop. Their lives become a living hell, just like an alcoholic's does. Their obsession starts to destroy their lives and the lives of everybody around them.

Now, all of this happens not just because they have a physical reaction when they eat certain foods, but because they have a mental obsession to eat them. There is another fellowship, called Overeaters Anonymous, which uses the Twelve Step program to help people overcome their obsessions with certain foods.

There is also a fellowship of people who are obsessed with gambling, called Gamblers Anonymous. It uses the same Twelve Step program to overcome not a physical problem, but an obsession with gambling. We have known some obsessive gamblers in our time, and their lives are exactly like those of alcoholics who are still drinking. They go on gambling binges and lose all their money; then they feel remorseful and swear they'll never gamble again. But sooner or later, they start feeling restless, irritable, and discontented. Their obsession kicks in, and their minds convince them to make just one two-dollar bet. Sure enough, pretty soon they can't stop, and they're caught in the cycle again. Their obsession starts to destroy their lives and the lives of people around them.

There is another group of people who are obsessed with, of all things, stopping other people from drinking. This is no joke—it's a very real obsession, and is very serious. It is exactly like the obsession that alcoholics, and compulsive gamblers, and compulsive overeaters have. These people will try every known way to stop other people from drinking alcohol. They'll have them put in jail. They'll run them through the divorce courts. They'll take their car keys away. They'll throw people who drink out of the house, put their clothes out on the porch, and then move them back in at midnight. They'll try everything in the world to stop another person from drinking. And guess what? In the process, they destroy their own lives and the lives of everybody around them. Their obsession makes their lives a living hell. Finally, they swear off getting other people to stop drinking. They stop chasing after people for a while, but pretty soon they get restless, irritable, and discontented. Their minds begin to search for a way to feel comfortable again, and their obsession kicks in, and pretty soon off they go again. They are exactly like alcoholics.

It all comes down to this: All obsessions are pretty much the same. The fact that we're allergic to alcohol isn't what's most important. The important thing is that we have an obsession in our mind, and whatever that obsession might be, the only way to recover is through the mind itself. That means finding a way to live without drinking, or gambling, or overeating, or whatever. This is the real problem not only of alcoholics but, in some form, most of the human race today.

The Need for a Psychic Change

p. xxvii,
ll. 7-9

If we look again at what Dr. Silkworth wrote on lines 7-9 of page xxvii, we are reminded that to recover from our obsession with alcohol, we have to experience a complete psychic change. If we could find a way to feel comfortable—instead of restless, irritable, and discontented—without drinking, then it wouldn't be necessary for us to drink. Dr. Silkworth says that we can find a way to feel comfortable by experiencing a psychic change, a change in our mental attitude and our outlook on life.

p. xxvii,
ll. 10-16

Since you can't do anything about your body's allergy to alcohol, your recovery will have to come about through your mind. The doctor explains on lines 10-16 of page xxvii that once a psychic change has taken place, the very same person who seemed hopeless before has no trouble controlling the urge to drink. The only thing necessary is following a few simple rules—the Twelve Steps.

In the chapters to come, we'll look at the Twelve Steps in detail, and show you exactly how to use them as a design for living sufficient for your recovery.

CHAPTER SIX

Learning from Bill W.'s Story

We have spent most of the first five chapters of this book describing the problem of alcoholism in detail. We went into so much detail because you can't find a solution to your alcohol problem, or any problem, until you fully and clearly understand what the problem is.

As alcoholics, our problem is not weak will, not moral character, and not sin. *Our problem is that we have an actual twofold disease: a physical allergy that ensures that we'll eventually lose control when we drink, and an obsession of the mind that makes us want to keep drinking.*

We cannot do anything about the physical allergy. That will stay with us for the rest of our life. Therefore, our recovery has to come through our mind.

Nevertheless, left solely to our own resources, we are powerless over alcohol. *And because we are powerless over alcohol, our lives have become unmanageable.*

This statement of the problem is Step One of the Twelve Steps.

On pages 59 and 60 of the Big Book are the Twelve Steps. pp. 59-60 (The Twelve Steps are also listed at the end of this book on page 172.) These form a complete, practical program of recovery for anyone suffering from the disease of alcoholism or other addictions. We'll return to the Twelve Steps frequently in our book. Right now, we'd like you to simply read them through slowly and carefully.

■ ■ ■

Step One says, "We admitted we were powerless over alcohol—that our lives had become unmanageable." That's our problem.

Now, to solve our problem of powerlessness, we need to find a Power greater than ourselves. The remainder of the Twelve Steps describe this solution and show us exactly how to find such a Power.

The Story of Bill W.

Chapter 1 of the Big Book is devoted to Bill W.'s story. First and foremost, it's the story of an ordinary man who found a solution to the problem of alcoholism. Bill W.'s experience informs and reassures us that our problem has a practical solution, and that this solution can be used by ordinary alcoholics like ourselves.

Bill W.'s story also serves as an example of everything Dr. Silkworth wrote about in "The Doctor's Opinion." It is a case history—a specific example that demonstrates and illustrates a set of general principles.

pp. 8-16   Chapter 1 also includes all Twelve Steps. If you read pages 8-16 carefully, you'll see that Bill W. proceeds through all of the Steps, one by one. As you read this chapter, you can watch over Bill W.'s shoulder as he reaches and works each Step. It is through these Twelve Steps and his reliance on a Higher Power that he is at last restored to sanity.

It is easy to identify with Bill W. His story is much like that of many alcoholics. Certainly, the two of us have stories very similar to his; we can see ourselves in nearly every paragraph of Chapter 1. Bill W.'s story can give you inspiration and hope, as you see that even someone hopelessly addicted to alcohol, as Bill W. was, can recover. If he can, so can anyone.

The two of us writing this book are living proof of this truth. Twenty-some years ago we followed Bill W.'s lead and put the Twelve Steps into practice in our lives. As a result, neither one of us has taken a drink in over twenty years. We both had the same problem Bill W. had—and the same solution that worked for him worked for us.

Bill W.'s story has been the beginning of hope and the beginning of belief for millions of people. When the two of us first read it, we said to ourselves, *If Bill W. could recover, and we're a lot like he was, maybe we can recover too.* We could and did, and so can you.

Some people say they can't identify with Bill W. because he was a high-powered New York City stockbroker and speculator who had gone through law school. People think they're different from Bill because they're laborers, or housewives, or students, or because they're unemployed. These people forget that for years Bill W. was unemployed, too, because of his problem with alcohol. And this happened *after* most of his high-rolling deals in the stock market, not before. Not long after he was making big-money deals, he was out on the street, too obsessed with alcohol to make a living. No, Bill W. was nobody special. He was just like any one of us.

If you've read this far in our own book and have not yet read Chapter 1 of *Alcoholics Anonymous,* "Bill's Story," please read it now. It's a frightening, vivid, and detailed account of one alcoholic's descent into madness. It is also the inspiring and uplifting story of his complete recovery and his resulting physical, emotional, and spiritual health.

The Twelve Steps as a Natural Process

We won't repeat Bill W.'s story here. The Big Book tells it better than we can. But we would like to point out the spots at which Bill W. accepted each of the Twelve Steps, in order, and how those Steps led to his recovery.

Of course, at the time of his recovery, the Twelve Steps had not yet been conceived of as a recovery program or written down. But Bill W. went through them nonetheless, because *the Twelve Steps describe the natural process alcoholics and other people with addictions go through to recover.* The Twelve Steps are a description of the recovery process, not an artificial set of exercises.

p. 8 — We suggest opening a copy of the Big Book to page 8 now and observing with us how Bill W. came to realize and put into practice each of these Steps.

After years of drinking, of trying to solve his problem through sheer willpower, and of failing miserably, Bill W.

p. 8, ll. 8-12 — finally arrives at Step One. On lines 8-12 of page 8, he admits his powerlessness over alcohol and his realization that his life is utterly unmanageable.

pp. 10-12 — On pages 10-12, Bill W. describes his own process of coming to believe that a Higher Power could restore his

bottom p. 12 — sanity. On the second half of page 12, Bill W. details this crucial realization clearly, elegantly, and beautifully. This is Step Two.

Page 13 of the Big Book describes Bill W.'s personal

p. 13, ll. 6-8 — journey through Steps Three through Twelve. On lines 6-8 he embraces Step Three, humbly offering himself to God, as

p. 13, ll. 10-15 — he understands God. Immediately afterward, on lines 10-15, he takes Steps Four, Five, and Six: He takes a personal inventory of himself; he faces his wrongs and admits them to himself, another human being, and God; and he becomes ready to have God remove his defects of character. Step Seven, in which he formally asks this Higher Power to remove those defects, is clearly implied.

p. 13, ll. 15-20 — On lines 15-20, Bill W. takes Steps Eight and Nine: making a list of the people he had harmed, becoming willing to admit those wrongs directly to the people he had hurt, and vowing to make amends to all such people.

p. 13, ll. 21-33–
p. 14, ll. 1-2, 23-33–
p. 15, ll. 1-5 — On the remainder of page 13 and on pages 14 and 15 we can see Bill W. taking Steps Ten through Twelve: continuing to take personal inventory and admitting his wrongs; seeking through prayer and meditation to improve his contact with God, as he understands God; and practicing the basic spiritual principles of honesty, humility, and following the will of a Higher Power throughout his life.

On these few pages, we can actually follow Bill W. through each stage of his spiritual awakening and each stage of his recovery. And in these pages we see clearly that he did recover, and that the Twelve Steps do work—even for the most hopeless alcoholic or other addict.

Bill W. first encountered Step Two toward the end of November 1934, when his friend Ebbie visited and told him of his own spiritual awakening. He had taken Step One in the Towns Hospital during his second trip there, for withdrawal from alcohol. He took Steps Three through Twelve a couple of weeks later while in the hospital. He left the hospital three days after taking Steps Three through Twelve and never took another drink for the remaining thirty-six years of his life.

In the story of Bill W.'s crisis and recovery, we can see an example of exactly what Dr. Silkworth writes about in "The Doctor's Opinion." And here's what we think is so very important about Bill W.'s story: If you're an alcoholic or otherwise addicted, and you're desperate, and you want to stop drinking and using, and you've been trying to stop but it hasn't worked, then you can see yourself in the first part of Bill W.'s story. His story—the misery, the hopelessness, the failure—is the same as yours. But if you want to stop drinking or using other drugs and solve your problem, then you can believe that the second half of his story—his recovery, his spiritual awakening, his sobriety, and his many years of stability and happiness—could be yours as well. What happened to Bill W. can happen to you.

CHAPTER SEVEN

The Fellowship And Spiritual Experience

What is the AA Fellowship?

The people in the Alcoholics Anonymous fellowship, and alcoholics and other addicts in general, come from a wide range of religious, economic, social, political, and occupational backgrounds. We are from every conceivable walk of life. This is as true today as it was fifty-some years ago, when the Big Book was first published. In fact, Chapter 2 of the Big Book begins by reassuring us that people in AA are average folks from all parts of the country*—people just like you and us.

People come together to form groups because they have something in common. What people in AA have in common is alcoholism. If you get a group of alcoholics together and try to get them to talk about something other than alcoholism, more than likely it'll be hard to get a decent conversation going. Most of the people in AA would probably never get to know each other if it weren't for the fellowship. Their paths simply wouldn't cross.

There exists among people in AA a friendliness and understanding that is indescribably wonderful—wonderful

---

* Since the time Chapter 2 of the Big Book was written, AA has expanded beyond the United States to (in 1989) 118 countries worldwide.
—Editor

because AA manages to bind completely different people together. There is a lot of strength and support in AA. People suffering from the illness of alcoholism come to AA and receive strength and hope from other people who are recovering from the same illness. People in AA share a common problem, and a common solution: a vital spiritual experience that results from working the Twelve Steps.

One of the great things about the fellowship is that members who have been in AA for a while, and who have worked the Twelve Steps themselves, help to support new members. Once a member has a spiritual experience and a psychic change as a result of working the Twelve Steps, he or she becomes an old member and helps support the next new member. We have visited lots of AA groups, and we've seen this arrangement work over and over, and we hear from others how this same thing has been taking place in other Twelve Step fellowships like Al-Anon, Cocaine Anonymous, Gamblers Anonymous, Narcotics Anonymous, Overeaters Anonymous, and so on.

Misconceptions About the Fellowship

Alcoholics Anonymous, like these other Twelve Step organizations, can be a strong, effective *support group*. It is not a religion, not a cult, and not a club. We need to understand that it is a support group—nothing more or less.

Over the years, we've run into people who misunderstand this. They think the AA fellowship is everything, the be-all and end-all of recovery. They have made AA into something more than it really is, and we believe that, in the process, some of them miss the whole point of the fellowship.

Those first one hundred or so people who got together and formed AA fifty-some years back didn't have much of a fellowship to rely on. There were only about one hundred of them, and they weren't all even in the same town—some were in Akron, some in New York, and a few in other places.

They couldn't depend much on an organization or fellowship. *What they depended on was a Higher Power—the real Power of recovery—and the Twelve Steps.*

Nowadays we hear people say things like, "Go to ninety AA meetings in the next ninety days and things will be okay." There is nothing wrong with that, but we don't believe that going to a meeting a day is what AA is about. Those first one hundred or so people couldn't go to ninety meetings in ninety days.

The AA fellowship is very useful and important, but the fellowship alone is not enough. *You cannot recover from the disease of alcoholism simply by going to AA meetings*—any more than you can become a parent simply by going to PTA meetings. We believe the same holds true for other addictive behaviors and their corresponding Twelve Step fellowships.

Recovery doesn't happen by osmosis. *The great fact is, we have discovered a common solution to this disease, which is the spiritual experience that results from working the Twelve Steps.* Alcoholics Anonymous and other Twelve Step meetings can offer you support and help you to use those Steps in your daily life. But just coming to meetings will not bring about the psychic change Dr. Silkworth talks about in "The Doctor's Opinion"—the change that is necessary for your recovery. *If you truly want to solve your problem of addiction to alcohol or your other addictions, we believe you must actually work the Twelve Steps.*

In some alcoholism and other drug treatment centers, people aren't told much about AA except that they should go to meetings once they've finished treatment. And, especially if the treatment has helped, people really believe that's all they need to do. But the fellowship can never take the place of actually working the Twelve Steps yourself.

In this respect, the Twelve Steps and AA are no different from going to school. If you're in ninth grade and you want to be promoted to grade ten, it certainly helps if you go to classes regularly. But if you go to classes but never do any studying on your own, you're not going to learn very much, and you probably aren't going to pass ninth grade. Just showing up isn't enough.

p. 17   On page 17, the Big Book explains exactly what the AA fellowship is, does, and means. We believe that the more we stick to this description, and the less we try to make the fellowship into something it was never meant to be, the better off everyone in the fellowship is going to be.

Recognizing Alcoholism

p. 20, 1. 15–
p. 25, 1. 3   On pages 20-25, the Big Book paints a detailed and accurate picture of a typical alcoholic. Not every detail of that description will fit every alcoholic; but if you're an alcoholic, we'll bet that you'll find yourself somewhere in this description. We can certainly see ourselves in these pages—the way we used to be before we stopped drinking and began recovery.

In our opinion, one of the best things the United States government has done in the last few years is educating the general public about what alcoholism really is. Through this education, people are learning to spot the signs of the disease of alcoholism early on, both in themselves and in people they're close to. As a result, alcoholics today don't have to do and be every one of the things the Big Book describes to recognize themselves as alcoholics, or to be recognized as alcoholics by others. Nowadays, thank God, more people begin looking for a solution to their problems earlier, before things get too bad and they completely ruin their own lives and the lives of the people around them.

What Is a Spiritual Experience?

bottom half
p. 25   Now we'd like to focus on the second half of page 25. The title of Chapter 2 of the Big Book is "There Is a Solution," and on this half-page, the solution is spelled out for us as plain as day. You'll remember from "The Doctor's Opinion" that

Dr. Silkworth said that the key to recovery is a "psychic change," which is described in some detail on lines 16-24 of page 25.

p. 25, ll. 16-24

This psychic change is the result of a spiritual experience. You'll see on line 17 that there's an asterisk after the words "spiritual experiences." A footnote at the bottom of the page says that this term is fully explained in Appendix II, which is on pages 569-570.

p. 25, l. 17

Those two words, "spiritual experience," are extremely important to the Big Book—so important that Appendix II was added in the second edition to explain what those words mean. When the first edition of the Big Book was published, there was no asterisk and no explanation of what a spiritual experience was; the text simply said that you had to have such an experience, and that it was up to you to determine what it was and whether or not you'd had it. Understandably, a lot of readers of the first edition found this vague or confusing, so in the second edition the explanation on pages 569-570 was added.

pp. 569-570

One problem with putting an appendix in any book is that many people simply won't read it. But Appendix II is one of the most important sections of the Big Book. If you haven't read it yet, we suggest you put aside this book until you've read these two pages.

Appendix II answered a lot of people's questions and probably resulted in a huge collective sigh of relief. Some people had gotten the impression that a spiritual experience had to be sudden and overwhelming like Bill W.'s. Sometimes it happens that way, but usually it doesn't. Bill W. said that of the first one hundred people in AA, about 10 percent had sudden spiritual experiences. The other 90 percent had slower, more gradual spiritual awakenings—what psychologist William James called the "educational variety" of spiritual transformation. In this kind of transformation, you change gradually, over months or years, as you learn and apply the Twelve Steps to your life.

While sudden spiritual experiences continue to occur, we think the sudden, overnight changes are rare. For both of us, the transformation has been gradual; of the people we've worked with in the last eighteen years or so, we know only five who have had sudden spiritual experiences. These experiences are definitely real, but they don't happen often. Most people will have a gradual spiritual awakening.

We believe it's very important to understand that both types of spiritual awakening are fundamentally the same. One is no better than the other. One happens suddenly, the other gradually—but they both do the same thing: They produce a *personality change* that results in your recovery.

p. 569 The key concept in Appendix II—and, in many ways, in all of the Big Book—is *change.* On page 569 alone, the words *change, changes, upheavals, transformations, alteration,* and *difference* appear a total of nine times. Change is what the Big Book is all about.

p. 27, ll. 12-26 In Chapter 2, on page 27, lines 12 through 26, Dr. Carl Jung, one of the greatest psychiatrists of all time, also speaks of the great importance of change—the type of psychic change brought about by a profound spiritual experience. He refers to "huge emotional displacements and re-arrangements" that accompany such an experience. This is exactly what Dr. Silkworth was talking about in "The Doctor's Opinion" when he said "psychic change." It's evident that psychic change, personality change, spiritual experience, or spiritual awakening all mean the same thing: *change.*

Putting the Information Together

Let's review for a moment what various people knew before the Big Book was published and the AA fellowship began. Then let's look at how all of this information came together.

Dr. Silkworth knew that a psychic change was necessary, but he didn't know, at least at first, how to bring about such a change. Dr. Jung realized that a vital spiritual experience would cause such a change, and he tried to find ways to produce such an experience in his patients.

Dr. Silkworth fully understood the problem (Step One)—a physical allergy plus an obsession of the mind. Dr. Jung knew the solution (Step Two)—a spiritual experience that causes a profound psychic change—but didn't know a great deal about the problem of alcohol addiction. Neither of the two doctors had developed much of a treatment plan.

Meanwhile, the Oxford Groups of the early 1930s, which we talked about back in Chapter One, *had* come up with a treatment plan, which was a sort of primitive version of Steps Three through Twelve. But the people in the Oxford Groups didn't fully understand the problem of alcohol addiction or its solution.

Eventually, in bits and pieces, all of this information found its way to Bill W. He was the first person to know all of it—an accurate description of the problem, an accurate description of the solution, and a workable plan of action for recovery. We're amazed at the way everything Bill W. needed to know made its way to him.

Once Bill W. had this information, he and others put it all together into an effective, practical recovery program—the Twelve Step program. Then they put the information into a book called *Alcoholics Anonymous*. It was after publication of the Big Book that the fellowship, Alcoholics Anonymous, was formed to carry the message that this solution to the disease of alcoholism had been found.

The Big Book contains the exact information that you need to know for your own recovery.

In the next chapter, we'll take a look at some of the most essential—and most frequently misunderstood—pieces of information in the Big Book.

CHAPTER EIGHT

Sanity and Spirituality

What Does the Big Book Mean by Sanity?

In Chapter 3 of the Big Book, "More About Alcoholism," Bill W. tells us about three alcoholics he knew and the insanity they experienced in relation to alcohol. While reading this chapter, it's helpful to keep Step Two of the Twelve Steps in mind:

> Came to believe that a Power greater than ourselves could restore us to sanity.

Let's take a good look at this statement. First of all, if we have to be restored to sanity, this means that, at least for now, we aren't sane. Most of Chapter 3 of the Big Book is devoted to the insanity that stems directly from alcoholism.

This is an area we really need to focus on. A lot of people don't understand what the Big Book means by sanity and insanity. When they read Step Two, they say, "Yeah, I need to be restored to sanity because I do a lot of crazy things when I drink or do drugs." They think the Big Book is referring to what happens when they're drunk or high. But, actually, the Big Book is talking about a different kind of insanity: the insanity that takes control of us *before* we drink or use—the insanity that makes us take that drink or hit. The crazy things we do when drunk or stoned are caused by our reactions to alcohol or other drugs and are not insanity.

In Chapter 5 of this book, we talked about the obsession we alcoholics have with taking that first drink. We also talked about other kinds of obsessions that have nothing to do with alcohol but that operate in exactly the same way. The big problem with an obsession is that it keeps us from seeing the truth—from seeing things the way they are. Instead of the truth, we believe in a lie. Worse, we take action based on that lie, acting as if it were true.

If you think about it for a moment, believing and acting on a lie is a form of insanity. Our obsession to drink or use other drugs causes us to ignore the truth and embrace a lie. *Our obsession with alcohol or other mood-altering chemicals or behaviors makes us insane.*

How People Lie to Themselves

p. 30, ll. 6-10

Alcoholics tell themselves, believe, and act on a host of lies to protect their drinking. But on page 30 of the Big Book, lines 6-10, Bill W. explains the biggest and most dangerous lie of all: that somehow, someday we can control, limit, and enjoy our drinking—that we can drink like normal people. We know and you know that this is a lie. But the persistence of this lie is amazing. People have died trying to make it be true, or died trying to prove that it's true to themselves or others. That's the big problem with lies: No matter what you do, you can never make them true.

p. 30, ll. 13-14

In the very next paragraph, lines 13-14, Bill W. explains that any notion we have that we are like non-alcoholics, or someday will become like them, absolutely has to be destroyed. If we believe the lie that we can drink or use other drugs safely—or, worse, act on it—then we're suffering from a form of insanity. Bill W. calls the belief in this lie an "obsession," "illusion," and a "delusion." All three are forms of insanity.

If you go to a dictionary and look up the work *sanity,* you'll see that it means wholeness of mind. Now, a mind that is whole can see the truth about practically everything. People with a whole mind can make decisions based on the truth, and their lives usually run pretty well.

Insanity means that your mind is less than whole, that you can't always see the truth—or, if you can see it, you can't always act on it. Insanity doesn't necessarily mean you're a raving maniac, or that you need to be put away—it just means that you're not quite all there. When it comes to alcohol, we alcoholics definitely seem to be not quite all there. We may be very intelligent and perfectly sane in all other areas of our life. We may make the right decisions and take the right actions when it comes to everything except alcohol. But with alcohol, we have difficulty seeing the truth and acting on it. We believe we can safely drink, when the truth is that we cannot drink without getting into serious trouble.

Most of Chapter 3 of the Big Book is devoted to examples of people who believed the lie that they could safely drink. Now notice, all of them believed this lie *before* they took the first drink. It was this lie that convinced them to take a drink in the first place, and then the allergy took over and they couldn't stop. Their problems didn't start after they took a drink. *Their trouble began when they believed and acted on a lie, while they were sober.* The insanity appears in the *conscious, sober* mind of the alcoholic who drinks. It isn't something that only appears after the drinking starts. The retired businessman who, after staying sober twenty-five years, killed himself from drinking (described on pages 32 and 33 of the Big Book) is an excellent example. p. 32, l. 13– p. 33, ll. 1-3

Another fellow named Jim, whom Bill W. writes about and reflects upon (pages 35-38 of the Big Book), is another good example. Jim knew he had an obsession with drink, and he went to AA and made a beginning. He had a decent job as a salesman, and he was able to bring his family back together, even though he'd torn it apart earlier with his drinking. We believe that Jim took Steps One, Two, and Three of the Twelve Steps, but he never went beyond Step Three. He never had a spiritual experience and didn't try to enlarge his spiritual life. His problem was that Step Three was as far as he went. p. 35, l. 11– p. 38, ll. 1-25

The Importance of the Twelve Steps

What a lot of people forget about the Twelve Steps is that they're in a deliberate, organized, and carefully thought-out sequence. The Big Book's program of recovery includes *all* Twelve Steps. You can't just pick the three or four you like best. Furthermore, you can't do Step Three properly until you've successfully put Steps One and Two into practice in your life. You can't do Step Four until you've put Step Three into practice, and so on. Jim got into trouble because he got as far as Step Three and said, "I feel okay, and I've got a job, and my family's back together; this is far enough." That was a delusion, and pretty soon Jim fell prey to a much more serious delusion: that he could find a way to drink alcohol. He convinced himself that so long as he mixed it with milk and drank it on a full stomach, he could drink like normal people.

Now, clearly, when Jim came to this conclusion he

p. 37, l. 4 wasn't thinking straight. On line 4 of page 37, Bill W. calls it "plain insanity." Like so many of us alcoholics, Jim was able to think straight about everything but alcohol. Because of his obsession with drink, he fabricated a ridiculous lie—then he believed it and acted on it. He was insane when it came to alcohol.

p. 37, ll. 28-33– p. 38, ll. 1-18 On the bottom of page 37 and the top of page 38, Bill W. tells another story. This one is about an imaginary fellow who is addicted to jaywalking. He gets a rush from running out in front of moving vehicles. This is one of our favorite examples in the Big Book.

You can easily guess what becomes of this guy. At first he's lucky and manages to jaywalk without injury. But the odds catch up with him, and he's injured several times. Yet he still keeps running out in front of vehicles, and soon he's broken an arm. He swears off his dangerous habit, but then he goes right back to it and gets both of his legs broken.

He still won't give up jaywalking, and pretty soon he loses his job, his wife leaves him, and finally he ends up in an asylum. He just can't get the urge to jaywalk out of his head. He eventually gets out of the asylum, and that very day he runs out in front of a fire engine. It hits him and breaks his back.

Clearly, this fellow is insane. The Big Book calls him outright crazy on line 17 of page 38.   p. 38, l. 17

Now let's substitute the word "drinking" for "jaywalking," and we've got the life story of millions of alcoholics. Are they any less crazy than the poor guy who practically jaywalked himself to death?

Fortunately, a lot of alcoholics today are getting to AA and the Twelve Steps before they lose everything—their jobs, their families, and their lives. They're luckier—and smarter—than our nameless jaywalker.

The Central Role of a Spiritual Experience

Let's look back at Step Two once again:

Came to believe that a Power greater than ourselves could restore us to sanity.

So far in this chapter we've focused on the last part of Step Two: the need to be restored to sanity. But what is it that will restore our sanity for us? According to the Big Book, it's not inner strength, or will, or determination, or any human creation. None of these is enough. As human beings, we can't restore our sanity on our own. We need the help of a Higher Power, a Power greater than ourselves.

If you read Chapter 3 of the Big Book carefully, you'll see that it returns several times to the importance of having a spiritual experience. Bill W. mentions it in Jim's story on   p. 35,
lines 25-26 of page 35. It plays an important part in the story   ll. 25-26
of another alcoholic, a fellow named Fred, on lines 21-33 of   p. 42,
page 42. Fred seemed a completely hopeless case—until he   ll. 21-33
discovered that spiritual principles would solve all his problems, including his problem with alcohol. And the final paragraph of Chapter 3 has this zinger: *There is no mental*   p. 43,
defense against alcohol that alcoholics can find or apply on their   ll. 26-30
own. The defense has got to originate from a Higher Power.

pp. 30-43 You might want to reread Chapter 3 now. As you do, you'll see that everything in the chapter is leading up to the final paragraph.

■ ■ ■

Chapter 3 doesn't pull any punches. It says clearly that, except for a rare case here and there, the help of a Higher Power is essential to our recovery.

Now, this seems strange to a lot of people at first. For a while, when the two of us first got involved in AA, it certainly seemed strange to us. Because of how we were raised, when we heard words like "spiritual principles" and "Higher Power," all we thought of was hellfire and brimstone and sin. We weren't sure we wanted any part of that. Then, suddenly, we found ourselves faced with the idea that we were either going to have a spiritual experience or die. That's a heck of a dilemma to be in.

A lot of us alcoholics have questions and doubts about religion. In fact, many of us have spent a good portion of our time sitting around in bars arguing about religion. Maybe you've passed a church on Sunday morning and thought, *Look at those suckers going in there, kneeling down and praying to something they don't even really believe in. They're a bunch of hypocrites.* The last thing you want to do is turn yourself into some kind of religious fanatic.

That is why the very next chapter in the Big Book is called "We Agnostics." Remember, Bill W. was one of us. He knew us. He felt just like we felt, and he must have said to himself, "I'm going to have to write something about this idea of spirituality, or people are not going to be able to get past Chapter 3."

He ended up writing one of the greatest pieces of information on spirituality that we've ever read.

CHAPTER NINE

Faith Versus Belief

We are especially fond of Chapter 4 of the Big Book, "We Agnostics." This is where Bill W. describes, discusses, and explains spiritual experience in detail. We think his explanation is beautifully simple, straightforward, and sensible. When most people write about spirituality, they knock themselves out trying to prove God's existence; often, they alienate the reader in the process. But Bill W. doesn't take this approach at all. Instead, he gives us a simple little procedure to follow that allows each of us to find God, as we understand God, for ourselves. He doesn't get too complicated.

One of the strange things about alcoholism is that even though it's a terminal disease, it's possible to come out of it in better shape than when you first realized you had it. What makes this possible is the kind of spiritual experience talked about in Chapter 4 of the Big Book. Alcoholism—and practically any other addiction—is a unique disease because, with very few exceptions, a spiritual experience is the *only* thing that can overcome it.

In Search of a Spiritual Experience

To an atheist or an agnostic, having a spiritual experience may seem outright impossible. But let's think things through on this subject for a moment and see where we end up.

Once you've accepted Step One, admitting that you're powerless over alcohol and that your life has become unmanageable, you've realized that to continue drinking means disaster. So does continuing to rely entirely on yourself to stop drinking. Now if you already know that you can't rely on yourself, then your choices narrow down to either relying on some Power greater than yourself or being doomed to an alcoholic death. These aren't easy alternatives to face, but they're the only ones you've got. If you truly want to recover from the illness of alcoholism or other drug addiction, you've got to have a spiritual experience.

p. 44, ll. 16-24 Fortunately, having a spiritual experience is neither difficult nor unusual—even for atheists and agnostics. In paragraph three of page 44, the Big Book says that about half of all of those first one hundred members of AA were previously atheists and agnostics. Yet every one of them had a spiritual experience, stopped drinking, and recovered. This paragraph also says flat out that it isn't hard or unusual to have such an experience.

Once you've accepted Step One, you've realized that anything that comes from your own resources—will, effort, philosophy, morality, goals, or good intentions—won't solve your alcohol problem. Your human resources alone simply aren't sufficient. Step One now becomes the foundation of your recovery.

Step Two is the cornerstone laid on that foundation. In Step One, you become willing to change; Step Two involves believing that a change is possible.

Choosing to Believe

p. 45, ll. 13-15 Lines 13-15 on page 45 are two very interesting sentences, and they're two of the key sentences in the Big Book. First of all, they don't say that a Higher Power will be a sort of helper or useful assistant. They don't say this Power will help you solve your problem or enable you to solve it. *They say that this Power will solve your problem.* Furthermore, these two sentences say outright that the main purpose of the Big Book is to enable you to find this Power. From here through page 164, the Big Book doesn't talk a great deal about alcohol anymore. Instead, it focuses on how to find the Power that will solve your problem.

The simple procedure for finding that Power begins on line 14 of page 47. You begin by asking yourself a question: Do you believe, or are you willing to believe, in a Higher Power?

p. 47.
ll. 14-16

Let's look at this question carefully. It is based on the concept of *belief*. Believing is the beginning of anything we accomplish in our life. Belief comes before purposeful action and is the seed of those actions. If we don't believe something is possible, we usually won't even bother to try it. Believing comes first.

If you want to change, you have to first believe that you *can* change. That's what Step Two is about. In Step One you admit that you have to make a change; in Step Two you believe that such a change is possible. If you don't believe you can change, you won't.

Many people confuse belief with faith. But faith and belief are very different. Belief comes *before* an action or decision; faith only comes afterward, as the *result* of an action or decision.

Suppose you've just moved to a new town where you don't know anyone. One day your car starts to give you trouble, so you decide you'd better get it fixed. You knock on your neighbor's door, introduce yourself, and ask her, "Do you know of a good mechanic in town?" She recommends a fellow named Mel, and tells you, "Mel does good work. I've been taking my car to him for years." So you decide to take your car to Mel.

Now you've never met Mel, and you've only known the person who recommended him for about five minutes. But you decide to take your car to Mel because you believe that your neighbor is telling the truth and that she has reasonably good judgment when it comes to car mechanics. For the moment, at least, you also believe that Mel probably does do good work. You don't have any *faith* in Mel yet, only belief. But this belief is enough for you to make a decision and take action.

Let's say that Mel works on your car, fixes it correctly and promptly, and charges a fair price. You are pleased with his work, so when you have another problem with your car a year or so later, you take it back to him for repair. This time, though, you're going back to Mel on faith, not just on belief. You have faith that he can fix your car well, based on your actual experience.

We think a lot of people get into trouble with Step Two because they confuse belief and faith. They want or expect to have faith before they can start. *But you can't get faith before you start.* You can only start with belief. Faith has to come later. First you believe; then you make decisions and take actions; then, if your decisions and actions work, you can begin to develop faith—*then and only then.* Belief is the cause of your actions; faith is their result.

The Process of Success

p. 51,
ll. 19-21 In lines 19-21 of page 51, Bill W. mentions Christopher Columbus, who was a living example of someone who first believed, then took actions based on his belief, and then developed faith as a result. You probably know that in Columbus's time, some of his contemporaries believed the world was flat. But Columbus had the idea that it was a sphere. Now, he didn't know this for a fact, but he believed that it was true. Because of this belief, he made his first famous voyage, which later on changed the world—its maps, its economics, and the lives of millions of people.

What made all the difference was that Columbus decided to take action based on his belief; he decided to test his belief by actually making a voyage westward, beyond where anyone had ever sailed. Sure enough, after a few weeks of sailing, he got results from his actions—he reached land in the West Indies. Though he thought he had landed in Asia, he proved that the world was round.

Columbus made three more trips westward. But after his first trip, he wasn't operating on belief anymore. He and the sailors who went with him were operating on faith— faith that the world was round and that they wouldn't fall off the edge. They had this faith because of Columbus's discoveries on his first voyage.

Columbus followed a simple process—the process of success. It is the same process that you can apply to your own life, no matter who you are or what your circumstances may be. You can always use it to change yourself or your situation. It's as simple as this: First you have a belief; then you make a decision, take action, and get results based on that belief. Then, if you've gotten the desired results, you don't just believe anymore—you know. You have faith.

The Twelve Steps are set up according to this formula. In Step One, you become willing to change because you've come to realize that you're powerless on your own and can't change your situation by yourself. In Step Two, you come to believe in the possibility of change and in the possibility of a Power that can make that change happen. In Step Three, you make a decision based on that belief. In Steps Four through Eleven, you take action based on your belief and decision. And by Step Twelve, if not before, you've gotten your results—a spiritual awakening, a psychic change, and recovery from the illness of alcoholism.

There are Twelve Steps to recovery, but these break down to a much simpler process: believing, making a decision, taking action, and getting results.

Twenty-some years ago, both of us came to believe that a Power greater than ourselves could restore us to sanity. Today we *know* that there is such a Power and that this Power did restore both of us to sanity.

There is a huge difference between just believing something and *knowing* it, having genuine faith in it. When we first got involved in AA, we believed in the possibility of a Higher Power; today we *know* there is such a Power. Today we have faith—not based on any hope or wish, but on our actual experience.

We did the same thing Columbus did: We believed, decided, acted, and got results. You can do exactly the same thing. In fact, this is exactly what we and the Big Book are asking you to do. Believe, decide, act, and see what kind of results you get. Then base what you do next on these results.

What Is a Higher Power?

p. 55,
ll. 9-22 We think lines 9 through 22 on page 55 make up two of the most important paragraphs in the whole Big Book. These paragraphs show us exactly where our Higher Power dwells and where we can find it: deep within us.

When we were kids, we had this picture of God as a tall, elderly gentleman hanging around somewhere up in the sky. He had a golden halo around his head and sun rays shooting out of that halo. In those days, we thought that God actually had to be up in the clouds. But that's not what the word "Higher" in "Higher Power" means—it means something larger and more powerful than we are.

That there is a Power greater than our *self*—our individual ego—is as much a fact as our physical existence. This Higher Power has been here all our lives, and throughout the lives of everyone who has ever lived on this planet. It's nothing new. We can call it our conscience, our inner intelligence, the Spirit, the Supreme Being, or God. What we call it isn't important. But deep down in every man, woman, and child is a fundamental idea or awareness of this Higher Power. Most of us have experienced this Power from time to time—as an inspiration, a presence, or an intelligence. Often, it takes the form of a voice somewhere within us, usually deep down. The two of us have had such an experience many times.

Now if it's true that God dwells within each human being, that means that each of us has his or her own personal God or Higher Power. And each of us and our own Higher Power can come together in simple and understandable terms. You don't have to worry about whether the God of your understanding is the God of the Baptists or the Catholics or the Jews or the Hindus. You don't necessarily need a priest, a complex philosophy, or someone else's sanction to have a Higher Power. You don't even have to call your Higher Power "God."

You don't have to join any religion or call yourself a religious person. However, if you're a devout believer in a particular religion, that's fine too. You don't have to leave whatever church you belong to or convert to some other religion.

The Big Book is quite explicit about this. In lines 10 through 23 on page 28, the Big Book explains that there are many different ways in which faith can be acquired, and that people of all religious affiliations will find nothing in the Big Book or the AA fellowship that contradicts their own beliefs.

p. 28, ll. 10-23

For many people, this is a new understanding of God. And with this new understanding, they're ready and able to move ahead and take Step Three.

CHAPTER TEN

Self-Will

By now we've gone through Chapter 4 of the Big Book, and we've begun to understand what the book means when it talks about a "spiritual experience" and a "Higher Power." Now we're up to Chapter 5, "How It Works," which is where Bill W. begins to tell us how to get sober. We suggest that you stop now and read the beginning of Chapter 5 from the top of page 58 through line 20 on page 60. It has become traditional in many Alcoholics Anonymous groups to open meetings with this reading

p. 58–
p. 60, l. 20

■ ■ ■

Please make a note—at least make a mental note—that pages 59-60 are where you can find all of the Twelve Steps. Or, if you prefer, copy down the Twelve Steps and keep it with you for easy reference. (The Twelve Steps also are listed on page 172 of this book.) You're going to find yourself wanting to refer to one or more of these Steps often in the future.

The Twelve Steps are more than just a list of ideas or suggestions: they're a design for living. We think they show how we can live a fully spiritual way of life as well as it has ever been shown.

Deciding to Act

Now that you've admitted you're powerless over alcohol or another addiction and you've come to believe that a

Power greater than yourself can restore you to sanity, you're ready for Step Three, which is to make a decision to turn your will and life over to the care of that Higher Power.

p. 60, l. 21–
p. 62, l. 33 Let's look at Step Three more closely, beginning with the word "decision." This is one of the key words in all of the Twelve Steps and all of the Big Book, because it represents the link between understanding and action. To find a solution to any problem, you first have to understand what the problem is—but understanding alone isn't enough. You also have to act on that understanding. And to act you first have to *decide* to act. It's impossible to take any kind of action without first somehow, in so many words, saying to yourself, "This is what I'm going to do."

A decision without an action that follows it is essentially worthless. If you're hungry and you decide to eat, but you don't actually eat anything, you're not going to get any nourishment, and you're still going to be hungry. Your decision to eat was meaningless because you didn't follow it up with any action. The result is the same as if you hadn't made the decision at all. In fact, it's the same as if you had decided to do *the opposite* and go hungry.

A few years ago, we decided that we'd go to Los Angeles for a visit. But we didn't actually do anything about that decision—we didn't make hotel reservations, buy plane tickets, or even put the time aside. So, of course, we didn't go to LA. In the end, our decision to go was meaningless because we didn't follow it up with any action.

But then, about a year later, one of us decided once again to go to LA. This time, he packed up his car, got it gassed up, and drove west. Sure enough, after a few days he made it to LA—not simply because he decided to go, but because he took the action necessary to carry out that decision.

Step Three involves making a key decision—turning your will and life over to your Higher Power. Steps Four through Nine are the actions necessary to carry this decision out.

Turning over Your Will and Life

Now that we understand the word "decision," let's look at a couple of other words in Step Three. You are supposed to turn your *will* and your *life* over to your Higher Power. But what exactly is your will? If you think about it, you'll realize that it's nothing more than your mind and your thinking. Your will is this thing up in your head that tells you what to do.

What about life? Your life is your actions—the sum total of all the actions you've taken throughout your lifetime. It is all the actions that have made you who you are and have put you where you are at this moment.

We will tell you straight out that Step Three can be very frightening for some people, at least at first. When the two of us first came to AA, we were scared to death by it. Step Three asked us to turn our wills and lives over to a Higher Power, but we didn't know what that Power would want us to do or be. What if our Higher Power decided we were supposed to become missionaries in some godforsaken place we didn't want to go to at all?

One of us told his AA sponsor about this fear. The fellow just laughed. He said, "Look back through your life. All your life you've been a selfish, self-centered human being. You've always thought whatever you wanted to think, made whatever decisions you wanted to make, and taken whatever actions you wanted to take. Look where it's gotten you. The end result of thinking and deciding and doing whatever you wanted is that you almost destroyed your life and the lives of everybody around you. This is what you're afraid of giving up? Maybe if a Higher Power could direct what you're thinking, your thinking might become better. And if your thinking becomes better, then maybe your actions will become better—and then maybe your life and the lives of people around you will become better too."

Here's what else he said: "You've already realized that, left to your own resources, you don't stand a chance. You'll just keep thinking the way you've always thought, and you'll act the way you've always acted. You'll get the same results, and your life will keep on being a living hell. There's no way your Higher Power is going to make your life any worse than it is now—so maybe your Higher Power will make your life better."

The fellow was right, of course.

Turning your will and life over to the care of a Higher Power isn't usually quick or easy. You can't just do it in a moment. It takes a decision *and* a lot of actions and work to turn your life around. Certainly it was this way for us and for most other recovering alcoholics we know. If you've been living a life of self-will for years, it's very difficult to just say, "Okay, this seems like a dead end, so from now on I'll turn myself over to the care of my Higher Power." It's not like deciding to change your brand of coffee or toothpaste. For most of us it's not easy, and it takes time.

The Nature of Self-Will

We need to talk about self-will for a bit, because a lot of people misunderstand what it is and how it works. First of all, self-will is a part of everyone's life. We are not saying self-will is bad, and the Big Book doesn't say it is either. In fact, self-will is a God-given part of who we are. We wouldn't be complete human beings without it. A sense of self is necessary and vital in life.

Our instincts are all forms of self-will. We have instincts for survival, for food, for shelter, for companionship, for sex, and even for self-esteem and pride. If we didn't have these, the human race wouldn't survive. But when our basic instincts get too big and out of control, they become destructive to us and to others. *If our sense of self is not controlled, it becomes the single most destructive thing in our lives.*

Each of us is like a house. To make a house livable and complete, it needs utilities—running water, electricity, and perhaps natural gas. Most of the time, these utilities make your home more comfortable and your life more pleasant. But if one of these utilities gets out of control, you end up with a fire or a flood, and your house can be destroyed.

Our will and instincts are like the utilities in a house. When used properly, in the way they were intended to be used, they can make your life smoother and more fulfilling. But if they are uncontrolled, they can do terrible damage to yourself and to others. In fact, by far the single most destructive force on this earth is the unregulated will of human beings.

We can get ourselves into the worst trouble when we set goals for the wrong reasons. As children, most of us are taught to set goals and then to work hard to reach them. We are also taught that it's often necessary to make sacrifices to reach those goals. But when we reach a goal, suddenly we're rewarded—with money, security, sex, love, status, or the respect or approval of others. We are also rewarded with a feeling of success and achievement. It all feels wonderful.

There is nothing wrong with setting goals. But let's look at what can happen once we've achieved the goal we've set, whatever it might be. At first, it feels fantastic; we're on top of the world. But unfortunately, more often than not, this feeling doesn't last very long. A little while after we've gotten whatever it was that we wanted so badly and worked so hard to attain, we may find ourselves looking around and saying, "Is this all there is to it?"

So we set a new goal for ourselves, and we work hard and strive toward it. We eventually reach that goal, and it feels good again for a little while—but, like before, that feeling doesn't last very long. So we set another goal, and the whole process just starts all over again. It has become a treadmill.

The funny thing is that we're not very satisfied with actually reaching our goals. Instead, all this goal-setting and effort and striving seem to create within us an insatiable desire for more power, more recognition, more prestige, more sex, more whatever. Then we start feeling like we're not getting there fast enough; other people aren't giving us the rewards as quickly as we want them or in the way we think we ought to get them.

After a while, we might start taking a few shortcuts. Maybe we start doing a little lying, a little conning, a little manipulating. Of course, anytime we do this, we hurt other people, and they usually retaliate against us and create pain and suffering for us. And we wind up in pretty deep conflict with other people.

This cycle can occur with any one of our instincts, whether it's our instinct for social acceptance or financial security or sex or anything else.

Maybe it's prestige and the respect of others that you're seeking. Maybe you've managed to work your way up to being foreman or vice president. Plus, you're the head of the volunteer fire department and a member of the local school board. It's all pretty impressive stuff. But soon after you get to where you want to be, you find yourself wanting to be in a higher position. You want to appear still greater in other people's eyes.

Or maybe what you're striving for is financial security. After twenty years of hard work, you've got your house paid for, your car paid for, and some money in the bank. It feels good for a while—but you can't help noticing that your next-door neighbor is driving a new Cadillac, while you've got a three-year-old Chevrolet. Pretty soon you want a new Cadillac too.

Or maybe it's sex that interests you particularly. It feels great every time you have it. The only thing wrong with it is that it's temporary. Once it's over, it's only a matter of a little time before you get to thinking about doing it again. The next thing you know, you're thinking about doing it with different people in different places and in all different ways. Before you know it, you're doing it at the wrong time in the wrong place and with the wrong people. And the funny thing is, instead of satisfying you, it creates an insatiable desire for more of the same. Soon enough, you're hurting others in pursuit of your own desires; in response, they retaliate against you, and you find yourself suffering.

Whether it's prestige and respect, financial security or sex that you're after, you eventually find yourself tempted to hurt other people or get in their way as you pursue your own goals. If you give in to this temptation, most of these other people are going to retaliate, and pretty soon you'll be in the midst of pain and suffering.

Does any of this sound familiar?

It is plain to us that a life run on self-will can almost never be successful and happy. Left to our own resources, we find the fulfillment of our basic instincts to be pleasurable, yet so temporary and fleeting that we're driven to fulfill them over and over and over. Almost invariably we overdo it, and fulfilling our instincts becomes an obsession. And when we overdo it, we come into conflict with other people and cause them pain and difficulty. That robs us of any possibility of peace of mind. Instead of gaining anything, we end up robbing ourselves—and hurting others, to boot.

Here is what Dr. Silkworth said in "The Doctor's Opinion" at the bottom of page xxvi and the top of page xxvii in the Big Book: When we alcoholics are sober, we're restless, irritable, and discontented. Often, too, we're filled with shame, fear, guilt, and remorse. And here's the worst part: *Left to rely only on our own resources, we will always remain that way because of our instincts and our will.* p. xxvi, ll. 34-35– p. xxvii, ll. 1-3

But if we can let our Higher Power control our will and instincts so that they operate at the level they were intended to operate, then maybe we won't feel so restless, irritable, and discontented, and maybe we can live without so much conflict and without doing so much harm to others. Then we wouldn't have to feel the shame, the fear, the guilt, and the remorse that come from hurting others.

Finding Freedom from Selfishness

As human beings, every one of us has self-will. The point of Step Three is not to eliminate that will or to try to stop being human—that would just be another obsession, another form of insanity. Instead, the task is for each of us *to let our Higher Power be the director of our will.* If a Higher Power directs your will, then that Power will direct your actions.

And if that Power directs your actions, then it directs your life, and you can at last live with some peace of mind and serenity.

p. 62,
ll. 6-25

As the Big Book says on page 62, selfishness and self-centeredness are the causes of our troubles. Our troubles are basically of our own making. We cannot, however, solve them on our own. Our problem is that we let our self-will control what we do; the solution is to give over the control of our will to our Higher Power.

p. 14,
ll. 3-6

Look back at Bill W.'s story for a moment, at lines 3-6 on page 14. Here Bill W. at last came to the inevitable realization that he had to let go of his self-centeredness. His self-will had to be destroyed, and he had to turn everything over to his Higher Power, which he calls here "the Father of Light." He had to give up the two things he held dearest to his heart—the same two things all of us alcoholics hold dearest: alcohol and self-centeredness.

Most of people's emotional problems are the result of unrestrained self-will. We alcoholics have more than our share of this problem.

Above all, it is essential to your recovery that you be free from selfishness. If you cannot, your selfishness will kill you.

Only your Higher Power can free you from that selfishness. Our next few chapters will show you what you can do to find that freedom.

CHAPTER ELEVEN

All or Nothing

You Can't Hedge Your Bets

We said in the previous chapter that turning your will and life over to a Higher Power probably won't be easy or quick. What we didn't explain was *why* this is so. It is because the self-will rarely gives up without a fight.

By the time we've reached Step Three, most of us are quite ready to turn over our drinking or other addictions to our Higher Power. But at the same time, most of us want to stay in control of the rest of our lives. We're not ready to give everything over to a Higher Power yet.

When the two of us first made it to Step Three, we basically said to God, "We'd like you to take our drinking, but don't mess with the rest of our lives. Stay out of things like money and sex; we'll take care of those ourselves. You just handle the drinking part."

A Higher Power doesn't work that way, though. Your will and life are more than just your drinking problem; you're asked to turn *everything* over. Your Higher Power wants the whole ball of wax. If you say to your Higher Power, "I want you to direct my thinking when it comes to alcohol, but otherwise leave me alone," you're going to be just as miserable as ever. You have got to give up everything. It's all or nothing. Like it or not, that's the way things work.

It took us a long time to really know and understand this—but now it seems like the most normal, natural, reasonable thing in the world, and we see why that's the way it has to be. You can't hedge your bets with your Higher Power.

Think about it for a little bit. The Big Book told us in Chapter 5 that our problem stems from selfishness and self-will—not just in relation to alcohol, but in everything in our lives. This means that we need a Higher Power to redirect all our thinking, not just our thoughts about alcohol. And if that Power is going to be redirecting our thinking, we're certainly going to be turning over a lot more than just alcohol.

The Disease Versus the Symptom

Suppose you've got some kind of infection throughout your body. It's making you feel miserable all over, but mostly you have this big, painful lump in your neck. You could go to your doctor and say, "Doc, I've got this lump in my neck. Grab your knife and cut it out, would you?" That would get rid of the lump, but it wouldn't be very sensible. You would be a lot smarter if you said, "Doc, prescribe some antibiotic for me so that I can lick this infection and be well again." You're much better off getting rid of the whole disease rather than just the worst symptom.

Of course, no decent doctor is going to hack out the lump and put you back out on the street; the doctor will look for a way to help you regain your health. You need a Higher Power in the same way—not to cure one of your symptoms, but to work on the whole disease.

So, in the end, you've got to turn over everything—your will and your life—to your Higher Power.

Now, you don't have to start out this way—in fact, getting to this point normally takes some time and some faith—but it's eventually where you'll end up. We believe that your success with the rest of the Twelve Steps, especially Steps Four through Nine, depends a lot on just how much of your will and life you're willing to turn over to your Higher Power. The more you're able to turn over to your Higher Power, the better the Steps will work for you, and the more success you'll have.

Twenty-some years ago when both of us were still drinking, we gave our entire wills and lives over to alcohol.

Alcohol determined where we would go, what we would do, who we associated with, who we slept with, and how we spent our money. It directed practically every waking thought the both of us had for years. We gave up everything we had to alcohol. This seemed to come naturally to us.

Yet when we were asked to give our wills and lives over to a Power truly greater than ourselves, we were frightened. We were afraid of relinquishing our wills and lives—yet by having this disease we had already relinquished them to alcohol! If we had made half the effort in turning everything over to the care and direction of our Higher Power that we made in turning it all over to alcohol a few years earlier, we'd have saved ourselves a lot of pain and suffering.

We are very grateful that we were finally able to give everything over to this Power and be restored to sanity.

The Choice Is Yours

Like it or not, you're in the same position now. Your choice is between alcohol or some other addiction and a Power greater than you are. There are no compromises, no half-measures, and no in-betweens. In order to be completely relieved of the mental obsession to drink or use other drugs, which is part of your disease, you've got to decide sooner or later to let your Higher Power have the whole ball of wax.

The Big Book is quite explicit about this. Look at the final paragraph on page 25. It says that for real alcoholics, there are no middle-of-the-road solutions. There are only two choices: surrendering to alcohol or accepting spiritual help. p. 25, ll. 25-32

This surrender doesn't have to come suddenly or immediately, though. In fact, in most people it takes a while. But once a Power greater than yourself is directing your will and your life, your whole life is going to improve. And this, more than anything else, is what the Big Book is about.

CHAPTER TWELVE

Taking Personal Inventory*

Step Three—deciding to turn your will and life over to a Higher Power—is a vital and crucial part of your recovery. But this decision will have little or no effect unless you can follow it up with action.

Getting Unblocked

Once you've completed Step Three, one of the first actions you can take is to begin removing from your personality some of the things that block you off from your Higher Power. Most of these blocks will be quite familiar; they've been a part of you for a long time. They include resentment, anger, fear, guilt, remorse, and shame. They also include memories of things you've done to harm others that have not yet been set right.

Once you decide that you want your Higher Power to take over your will and life, it makes sense to clear these things out of the way so that the Power can work more freely

---

* This chapter, and the three chapters following it, can be read in a couple of ways. If you've just completed Step Three, you can use these chapters to guide you in completing your Fourth Step. If you've already done a Fourth Step, these chapters may give you further insight into what that experience can mean for your continuing recovery. Or you may find that you'll want to take another Fourth Step now or in the near future to more thoroughly prepare yourself for working or reworking the Steps that follow.

—Editor

in you. As long as these things are in your mind, a Higher Power cannot enter your mind and direct your thinking.

To clear these things out of the way, you first have to know and recognize what they are. This is the purpose of Step Four, in which you make a searching, fearless moral inventory of yourself.

People sometimes ask us, "When is the right time to take Step Four?" Our answer is always, "At once—right after you take Step Three." Taking Step Three usually moves enough self-will out of the way so that you're able to strike while the iron's hot and take Step Four immediately.

If you don't take Step Four right after working Step Three, it's easy to start saying to yourself, "I don't think I really need to do that. I'm really not that bad." But that's just your self-will talking—coming back in and blocking you from going on with the Twelve Step program. Once you've made it to Step Three, we believe you should jump right into Step Four as soon as possible.

A little while ago, we heard a recovering alcoholic tell people at a seminar that they should wait two years after taking Step Three before taking Step Four. We believe this is terrible advice, and we wonder how many people died because they followed it. Our guess is that it took the fellow leading the seminar two years to go from Step Three to Step Four, so he figured everybody should take two years too. But why not save yourself the two years and move straight on to Step Four?

Understanding Step Four

We think Step Four is one of the most misunderstood Steps. For one thing, some people who have taken Step Four like to play King of the Mountain with newcomers. They tell them how rough Step Four is, and say, "Boy, just wait till you get to it." They make it sound as scary as they can. The reality, though, is that Step Four is very simple, and there's nothing about it to be afraid of at all.

Another problem is that people tend to procrastinate. Our pride says, "You don't have to do this," and at the same time our fear says, "Don't you dare do it!" And the longer we procrastinate, the louder these two voices get.

The trouble with procrastination is that if you're still restless, irritable, and discontented, and if you're still filled with fear, guilt, remorse, and shame, then every day that you stay that way is one day closer to the day when you might take a drink or a hit. Even though you're going to Alcoholics Anonymous or other Twelve Step meetings, and even though you've already worked Steps One through Three, your mind might start pulling you back to the idea that taking a drink or some other drug will make you feel better. So every day you put off working Step Four could be a day closer to the time when you get drunk or high again.

People also tend to put off Step Four simply because they don't understand what it means to take an inventory of themselves. There are no instructions in the Big Book like, "First, take a pencil and a legal pad, and put the numbers one through twenty on the left." Actually, though, some very explicit instructions *are* right there in Chapter 5, and they're clear, simple, and easy to follow. In fact, they're so simple that our keen alcoholic minds often overlook them completely!

These directions begin on line 8 of page 64, and continue through the bottom of page 70. In these pages, Bill W.— referring to himself as "we"—explains exactly what he did to take his own personal inventory. All we have to do is follow along, see what he did, and do the same for ourselves. We suggest you reread these pages now.

p. 64, l. 8–
p. 70, l. 32

■ ■ ■

Instructions for Taking a Personal Inventory

As Bill W. explains in lines 8 through 16 on page 64, taking a personal inventory is just like taking a business inventory; the two work in the same way. A business inventory is fact-finding and fact-facing, regarding the truth about the stock-in-trade. A personal inventory is searching

p. 64,
ll. 8-16

and fearless regarding our morals—the truth about ourselves. Where the object of a business inventory is to disclose
damaged or unsalable goods and get rid of them promptly
without regret, a personal inventory is for doing the same
thing with our flawed thinking that produces resentment,
fear, and behavior that is harmful to others. On page 65, Bill
W. even provides part of a sample inventory for a hypothetical person.

ll. 8-30

We are often asked, "Is it okay if I take a personal
inventory in my mind, or do I have to write it down?" *We
believe it's essential that your personal inventory be in writing.* In
fact, the Big Book specifies in three places that we put our
inventory "on paper" (page 64, lines 28-29; page 68, lines 3-
4; and page 69, lines 16-17). We are regularly reminded to
refer back to our lists and, finally, on page 70, lines 23-24,
we're told outright that being thorough in our inventory
means having written it down. According to the Big Book, if
you're not writing things down, you're not really taking
inventory.

p. 64,
ll. 28-29
p. 68,
ll. 3-4
p. 69,
ll. 16-17
p. 70,
ll. 23-24

Now the very first thing Bill W. tells us about inventories
is that any business that doesn't take an inventory regularly
is likely to go broke. Suppose you run a shoe store and don't
bother to take inventory regularly. You wouldn't know
what you've sold, what shoe sizes and styles you need to
reorder, what goods have been stolen or damaged or are
unsalable, or what shoes people are buying or not buying.
After awhile, what you have in stock wouldn't match what
people want to buy. Sooner or later, you'd probably
go broke.

We alcoholics are each in the business of staying sober.
For us, this is the most important business in the world. If we
don't inventory our "business" regularly, we won't be aware
of our flawed thinking that's blocking us from our Higher
Power, and we could end up "going broke." For alcoholics,
going broke means going back to drinking.

The most important part of taking any inventory is
finding the facts and facing them fearlessly. Let's return to
the example of a shoe store. Suppose you've got three

hundred pairs of saddle shoes in stock, and no one wants to buy them because they're out of style. If you ignore the facts and say to yourself, "These saddle shoes are real beauties, so I think I'll order four hundred more pairs," pretty soon your business is going to go belly up.

It's the same with a personal inventory. If you're not honest with yourself and if you start writing down things that aren't true, pretty soon you're going to be in trouble. You will be running your business into the ground instead of making it stronger and healthier.

It is important that you stick to the truth if you really want to recover from your addiction to alcohol or other drugs, even if facing the truth seems painful at first. You have got to collect truthful and complete information, and then you've got to look at that information squarely and honestly. A truthful inventory is the same as a moral inventory.

Let's consider that hypothetical shoe store a bit more. Suppose that you've just taken inventory, and you've come up with some pairs of shoes that are damaged, some that are clearly out of style, and some others that are unsalable. Obviously, these shoes are of no use to you just sitting there in your inventory—in fact, they're taking up space for shoes that people would actually buy. You need to get rid of these damaged and unsalable items promptly and without regret.

You already know that you're in the business of staying sober. And what you think and do determines whether or not you're going to stay sober. So, in taking your personal inventory, you need to find those "damaged and unsalable goods"—those thoughts and actions that block you from your Higher Power and may cause you to take a drink or get high. Once you've located these flawed or damaged thoughts and actions, you need to get rid of them promptly and without regret.

If you can get rid of the thinking that blocks you from the will of a Power greater than yourself, then the thinking that reflects the will of that Power can take its place—and you can be sober, peaceful, happy, and free, instead of restless, irritable, and discontented.

Focusing on Today

A lot of people think you have to wait until you've worked Step Twelve to get much of anything out of the Twelve Steps and the Big Book. *We think this is absolutely untrue.* Working each one of the Twelve Steps offers a positive experience—something you can feel and profit from. If you're like most people, you will feel better with each Step you take.

We also think Step Four is one of the biggest Steps; big changes start to happen as soon as you begin to put it to work. Most people start feeling a lot better as soon as they've finished working Step Four. This means that you can start feeling the real benefits of the Twelve Step program today.

Remember, too, that Step Four (making a searching and fearless moral inventory of yourself) is based on your thoughts and actions today—not next week, not two years from now, and not twenty-five years ago. If your thinking is solid and clear today, you'll probably still be sober tomorrow, and you'll "stay in business." But if your thinking today is off track, and you've blocked yourself from your Higher Power, then you could "go broke" and get drunk tomorrow. So you've got to look at your thoughts and actions as of *right now* and get rid of whatever is "damaged or unsalable."

We have found that for just about every alcoholic or addict these flawed or damaged thoughts fall into three categories:

1. Resentments and anger
2. Fear
3. Guilt, remorse, and shame

We have noticed time and time again how our Higher Power works. Our Higher Power gave each of us self-will, which we can use as we please until we die. Our Higher Power will never take that will away from us until we surrender it ourselves. If we want to, we can use that will to drive ourselves crazy, or drink ourselves to death, or anything else we choose. So long as we cling to our self-will, our

Higher Power is never going to take it away from us. We can just keep stewing in our own juice. This route leads to disaster. If you want to get rid of your flawed or damaged thinking, you've got to *give it back to your Higher Power, voluntarily, on your own.* Only when you give back your will and your thinking, and ask your Higher Power for saner thinking, can your flawed or damaged thought patterns be taken away.

Once your flawed or damaged thoughts have been removed, you will see that they were what was blocking you from your Higher Power, and that you can now begin to follow your Higher Power's will and directions.

Getting Rid of Resentment

All of us have felt resentment, but most of us have never stopped to analyze our resentments. We have spent plenty of time looking at what other people have done to us; we've gotten angry at them, and maybe we've spent some time figuring out how to get even with them. But that's as far as most of us have gone. We have never really looked at our resentments or at what caused them, nor have we tried to figure out how to get rid of them. Most of us never even thought of trying to get rid of them; instead, we tend to cling to them. Most of us cherish our resentments and even feed them like they are some sort of special pet.

Now that you've decided to get rid of your flawed or damaged thinking that blocks you from your Higher Power, you'll realize that your resentments and anger have got to go. From everything we've seen in working with many people over the years, *resentment destroys more alcoholics than anything else.* This isn't just our observation. Lines 23-24 on page 64 of the Big Book say exactly the same thing: resentment is the number-one offender. Thus, we feel it's extremely important that you begin by focusing on resentment when you take your personal inventory. If you can write down your resentments and look at them honestly, you'll be

p. 64, ll. 23-24

a lot closer to getting rid of them. Chapters 5 and 6 of the Big Book will show you exactly how to get rid of your resentments and how to keep them from coming back in the future. (We will discuss this in detail later on in this chapter and in the chapter that follows.)

The Nature of Resentment

Resentment is destructive when it means to persistently re-feel old pain—our anger, hurt, and indignation from the past—by replaying and reliving our memories of the incidents that caused the pain.

We need to understand that resentment can be a natural feeling and a natural process. All of us have some resentments. In fact, in some situations where resentment takes the form of righteous indignation, it can play a useful role. For one thing, this kind of resentment can make us get up and act. Imagine that you live in a somewhat run-down neighborhood. Your home needs painting, but all the other homes on the block do too. So you aren't particularly bothered by the peeling paint and ratty appearance of your house, and neither are any of your neighbors.

Now suppose a new fellow moves into the neighborhood. He buys the house right across the street from yours, and after a few days you see him painting his house and putting in new windows. Now his house looks a lot better than yours. You resent that, so you paint your house and put in some new windows and a new door.

Now your neighbor gets resentful because at this point your house is nicer than his, so he landscapes his front lawn and builds a patio. This makes half the homeowners on the block resentful, and pretty soon they're all out painting their homes and laying sod and building patios of their own.

This type of resentment can be useful, because it encourages a form of *constructive* competition. But what happens more often, especially among us alcoholics, is that our resentment gets used negatively, to make matters worse or more painful instead of better.

For example, let's imagine an alcoholic couple named Sue and Ralph. Sue and Ralph live on the same block where people are competing to see who can do the best fix-up job on their home. But instead of joining in and remodeling their house, Sue and Ralph let it stay as run-down as ever. As homes on the the block improve, Sue and Ralph start to get angry at their neighbors, and they allow their house to look worse and worse by comparison. Pretty soon, their house is the eyesore of the block, and they resent the hell out of all their neighbors. Eventually, they stop talking to them, and when a group of neighbors offers to help them repaint their house, Ralph yells at them, "Get off my property!" Then, of course, he goes inside and he and Sue start drinking.

In this case, Ralph and Sue used their resentment to turn a potentially positive and constructive event into something negative. Then, once they made the event negative, they used their resentment to make it even more painful. That is what we alcoholics often do with resentment.

Many of us even go a step further. We take a painful incident and we replay it over and over in our heads—for hours, days, months, and even years. We feel the pain a second time, and a third time, and maybe a thousandth time. We alcoholics are particularly good at this. We say to ourselves, "I don't know why I got hurt. I wasn't doing anything. Somebody just came up to me and hurt me." And then we replay the whole thing over so that we can feel the pain again. It should come as no surprise that the pain hurts just as much each time—maybe more. The stupidity of this is that while somebody else may have hurt us originally, we are now hurting ourselves each time we replay the incident in our minds.

So right now Sue is probably sitting in her living room, reliving over and over the time her neighbor's son called her "witch lady." And Ralph is recalling the time the man across the street told him to keep his dog out of his yard. Or the time the city housing inspector cited him for several housing code violations. Poor Ralph and Sue have got dozens, maybe hundreds, of these little videotapes in their heads, and they play them over and over and over. The result is that they are both effectively blocked off from their Higher Power.

On top of that, what most of us do, without realizing it, is to change what happened each time we replay the event. Again, alcoholics are especially talented at this. We embellish and dramatize things a little bit more each time: Maybe we make ourselves a little bit more virtuous, and the people who hurt us, and the things they did to hurt us, a little bit nastier. Eventually, when we replay the incident, we've changed it so much that it hardly resembles what actually happened.

We don't deny that people have done things that hurt you. People—some more than others—do things that hurt other people. That's a simple fact. Life isn't always easy, and we don't know of a way to keep these things from ever happening. So long as you're alive, you're going to get hurt sometimes.

But look at what alcoholics do: Every time they get hurt, they hang on to that hurt, and they replay it over and over. It's like they've got a replay machine in their heads. And here's the weird thing: They don't use that replay machine to record the good things that happen. They only record the painful things. So it's no surprise that when they turn the machine on and begin playing things back, all they see are painful incidents.

Let's follow our suffering acquaintance Sue on a bad day. She wakes up, turns on her mental replay machine, and records all the bad stuff that takes place during the day. Then when she gets home at night, she replays all of the painful incidents. They're awful, and she makes herself sick.

Now here's the strange part: Let's follow Sue on a *good day*. She wakes up and goes through her day with the replay machine turned off most of the time: She only turns it on once or twice, when things are going badly. Then she gets home and replays one or two bad things that happened that day—plus some other bad things she's saved from days, weeks, months, and years past. And guess what? She feels awful and makes herself sick!

This kind of resentment is like a boomerang—it goes out and then it comes right back at you. This is why it can be such a terrible, destructive thing. Once you resent someone long enough, sooner or later you'll resent your own position in life—and then you'll resent yourself for letting yourself get into that position. You end up swimming in self-pity.

Eventually, some of us start to live off resentment and self-pity. They become the guiding forces in our life.

Does this sound familiar? This pattern of resentment, self-hatred, and self-pity is extremely common among us alcoholics and among other drug addicts. It's one of our biggest problems, and it often becomes a seemingly natural part of how we think. But actually it's not natural at all—it's a form of sick thinking we've created for ourselves.

One of the worst things about resentment is that whenever you're busy resenting somebody or something, at that moment that person or thing is controlling your will and your life. And if other people and things are controlling your will and your life, that doesn't leave any room for direction from a Power greater than you are. Your Higher Power can't direct a mind that is being controlled by resentments

Putting Your Resentments on Paper

Lines 28-31 on page 64 of the Big Book explain exactly what Bill W. did to take his personal inventory. He listed on paper all of the people, institutions, and principles he was angry at. To begin your inventory, we suggest that you do exactly the same thing. p. 64, ll. 28-31

On page 65 of the Big Book, you can see exactly how Bill W. listed his resentments in three columns. The example he uses lists the resentments of an imaginary person, but the list is presented in exactly the same format that Bill W. used. p. 65, ll. 8-30

This format has worked well for all kinds of people, so when you're ready to do your Fourth Step (or, when you're ready to do Step Four again if you've already done it), you can take some paper and a pen or pencil and follow Bill W.'s instructions. First, turn the paper on its side so that it's wider

p. 65, l. 8 than it is long. Then make three columns. Title the first column (which will take up the left third of the paper)

I'm resentful at:

Title the second column (which will take up the middle third of the page)

The Cause

And title the third column (which will take up the right third of the page)

Affects my:

So, these will be the headings of your inventory chart for your resentments:

I'm resentful at: *The Cause*   *Affects my:*

■ ■ ■

Then you can start filling in your inventory chart. Be sure to start with column one, *(I'm resentful at:)*. Don't worry about the other columns yet; we've found that it's easiest to take a personal inventory by dealing with one column at a time. Leave about an inch of vertical space between each of your resentments in column one so that you'll have enough room to fill in the other two columns later.

In column one, write down all the *people* you feel resentful toward, whether they're alive or dead. List them all, however few or many there might be.

■ ■ ■

Then list any *institutions* you resent—the police department, the IRS, the post office, the church, or whatever.

■ ■ ■

Then list any *principles* you feel resentful toward—laws, moral codes, household rules, the Ten Commandments, the three laws of thermodynamics, Murphy's Law, "as ye sow so shall ye reap," etcetera.

■ ■ ■

It might take you awhile just to make a list of the people and things you resent. That's fine. You may end up with several pages of resentments—maybe even a little book. What's important is that your list is thorough and complete.

On page 65 of the Big Book, Bill W.'s imaginary alcoholic lists four of his resentments as examples. We doubt seriously if many real alcoholics are only angry at four or five people and things. When we did our own first inventories, twenty-plus years ago, we were amazed at how many people, institutions, and principles we were mad as hell at. p. 65, ll. 9, 15, 21, 27

It is sometimes hard to get started on this list. God knows we had trouble at first when we had to do our inventories. One of us started off by saying, "Hell, I don't have any resentments," but pretty soon he could think of three or four, and then five or six. By the time he was finished, he had a list of 162 people, institutions, and principles he was angry at. It turned out that he was mad at almost everything, but until then he hadn't known it. That's the way it sometimes is with resentments. Few of us realize just how fully resentments control our thinking and our life until we put them all down on paper. You can only see one resentment at a time in your head.

So getting started might be tough, but it gets progressively easier once you've started writing. We can tell you this too: We have never met an alcoholic yet who doesn't know exactly who and what he or she is mad at. After all, alcoholics spend thousands of hours sitting around in bars talking about their resentments!

Once you've finished with column one, you're going to realize just how much resentment controls your thinking and your mind. If resentment controls you, then a Higher Power cannot direct you. Now move on to column two (*The Cause*). Once again, don't worry about filling in the third column for now. Just go down column two from top to

p. 65,
ll. 9-30

bottom, one item at a time. Look at each of your resentments; then, in a few words, write down its cause or causes, just like Bill W.'s imaginary alcoholic did on page 65 of the Big Book. There may be one cause or, in some cases, multiple causes.

■ ■ ■

Once you've finished with column two from top to bottom, put down your pen or pencil and look over the causes of each of your resentments.

If you're like the vast majority of alcoholics and other addicts, you're going to see something amazing. You'll see that you're upset at just about all of those people, institutions, and principles not so much because of what they are but *because of what they did to you.* It's not the people or things that got you upset—it's what they did.

p. 65,
ll. 27-30

Look at the sample inventory on page 65 of the Big Book again. Bill W.'s imaginary alcoholic isn't mad at his wife because she's his wife or because she's tall or has freckles— he's angry because he thinks she misunderstands him, nags him, has her eyes on Brown, and wants the house to be put in her name.

p. 65,
ll. 9-14

Let's suppose for a minute that Mr. Brown did none of the things listed in column two, but that Mr. Green did them instead. Would Bill W.'s hypothetical fellow still be resentful of Mr. Brown? Of course not—he'd resent Mr. Green instead. In fact, no matter if you change any of the names and people in this inventory, Bill W.'s imaginary fellow is going to be just as mad—only he'll be mad at different people.

You can do the same with the items on your own list of resentments and causes. In each case, it's not the person, institution, or principle that got you mad—it's what he, she, or it did to you. Chances are you'd be just as upset if a different person, institution, or principle did exactly the same thing to you.

Now let's move on to the right-hand side of the page. In column three (*Affects my:*), write down exactly what part or parts of you got hurt. Opposite each name in column one and each cause in column two, list the area or areas of your life that were threatened or damaged by what this person, institution, or principle did.

People get angry when their instinctive needs for social belonging and acceptance (including self-esteem, pride, and nurturing relationships), security (both emotional and material), and sexual relations (both acceptable and hidden) are threatened. In almost every case, we've found that one or more of these basic life issues that define our sense of *self*, including our ambitions, have been interfered with in some way. We can list these issues for use in completing column three *(Affects my:)* as:

1. Self-esteem
2. Pride
3. Personal relationships
4. Material security
5. Emotional security
6. Acceptable sexual relations
7. Hidden sexual relations
8. Ambitions

Acceptable sexual relations are those that won't harm you or someone else and aren't in conflict with your values. *Hidden sexual relations* are those you have to keep quiet from someone—your wife or husband, for example. For a lot of married alcoholics, it means having sexual relations with someone else on the side.*

Ambitions are our plans for the future.

In the case of Bill W.'s imaginary alcoholic, every one of his personal injuries fits into one of these eight basic life issues. We expect that the same will be true in your own inventory.

p. 65, ll. 9-17, 21-22, 27-29

---

*This of course, does *not* include sexual abuse—any sexual behavior that was forced on you against your will, either as a child or as an adult. As with any abuse you may have suffered, it is important to feel your anger and not fault yourself. You may need to seek qualified professional counseling to work through traumas like these. Do what you must to rid yourself of this resentment so that the person who hurt you no longer controls your thoughts and actions. If other people are still directing you, your Higher Power can't.

—EDITOR

As you fill in column three from top to bottom, keep this book open to the list of the eight basic life issues in which you've been hurt (page 99). Refer to this list as often as you like. If you prefer, copy the list on a separate page. As you fill in column three, you'll soon see that, for each entry under *The Cause*, you can simply pick the appropriate item or items from the list in this book and write them down in column three.

■ ■ ■

It should go without saying that you need to be entirely honest about everything in your inventory. If you're pretending to yourself or avoiding the truth, you're only getting in your own way. *You can't give up your resentments unless you're first willing to honestly admit them and face them.* Remember that Step Four calls for a *searching and fearless* moral *(truthful)* inventory of yourself—not a lukewarm or half-measured one.

The Source of Anger

After you've finished filling in column three, put down your pen or pencil and take a short break.

■ ■ ■

Look over your inventory chart carefully from beginning to end.

You are going to notice certain patterns. For example, you might see that many or most of your grudges are against members of your family. You might realize that many of the causes of your resentments, listed in column two, have to do with your work. You might see that things that have to do with self-esteem or hidden sexual relations or emotional security show up a lot in column three. *This inventory will help you see where your anger and resentment really come from.*

Before either of us stopped drinking, we had no idea where our anger came from. We would get angry and then immediately act on that anger, and we wound up doing things we were sorry about later on. Then we'd apologize and say things like, "I'll never do that again." But the next time when something similar would happen, we'd get mad and do the same things all over again. We couldn't do anything about our anger because we didn't know where it came from. We'd just feel sore and then react.

Today we know that anger comes as a reaction to a threat or a perceived threat to one of our basic life issues. Sometimes we can prevent threats or keep them to a minimum. Sometimes, though, we can't stop them or limit them, or even slow them down.

But we *can* do something about how we react to threats. We can't change people or what they do, but we can change our response.

Anger and Blame

In making your personal inventory, you learned three very important things. First, you learned from column one that anger and resentment really do control you. Second, you learned from column two that it's not people, institutions, and principles that make you angry and resentful—it's what they did to you. Third, you learned from column three that you get angry because one of your instinctive needs has been threatened.

You can change how you respond to threats; you don't have to respond with resentment and anger.

In the sentence that begins on the very last line on page 65 and continues at the top of page 66 of the Big Book, Bill W. comes right out and says that the world and the people who live in it are often wrong—in fact, sometimes very wrong. But most of us stop right there; we don't go any deeper. We just say, "Yeah, they're awfully wrong, and I'm mad as hell about it."

p. 65, l. 33–
p. 66, l. 2

p. 66, ll. 2-3

That's the way the two of us used to think. We would blame others, get sore and stay sore, and sooner or later we'd get sore at ourselves, to boot. Then we'd retaliate and try to get our own way, but that would just make things worse. So we'd replay those resentments over and over, wasting our time and our lives over them—and making ourselves sick and miserable in the process.

The strange thing about all those resentments is that they don't do anyone any good. They don't make anyone any money. They don't straighten up a relationship with another human being. They don't increase anyone's confidence or serenity or security or happiness. They only make things worse.

There was a time when both of us spent much of our waking lives being angry at other people. Whether we were drinking or sober, we spent hour after hour replaying our resentments over and over. That time we spent was absolutely wasted.

In our recovery, we learned to let go of our resentments and anger. We are no longer mad at other people, or at ourselves, and it feels great. We're sober, peaceful, happy, serene, and free, instead of resentful, restless, irritable, and discontented.

Which way would you rather feel?

The Bottom Line on Resentment

Once you've finished your written inventory, look back at your list of resentments again. This inventory holds the key to your future. It is there for you to turn to and look back on whenever you need it to help you let go of your resentments and anger.

In the past, when you thought about the people and things that angered you, you'd think about all the hurtful things they did to you. Starting right now, we'd like you to look at your inventory from an entirely different angle: *Look at what each of your resentments has done to you.* Here's what we think you'll find:

Each of your resentments has made you miserable and unhappy; each has closed you off from the will of your Higher Power; and worst of all, each has caused you to drink or use other drugs.

According to the Big Book, the very worst thing about resentment is this: If you don't do anything about it, it'll kill you. It blocks you off from your Higher Power. It won't just ruin your life—it'll end it. Lines 13-19 on page 66 of the Big Book say it flat out: Resentment is fatal. You already know what happens once you start to drink, and you also know that, for an alcoholic or addict, continuing to drink or use leads to insanity or death. Once your resentments and anger cause you to take a drink or use, you're on the road to disaster. p. 66, ll. 13-19

It all boils down to this: *It doesn't matter whether your resentments are justified or unjustified.* The fact is that your resentment and anger block you off from the will of a Higher Power, and they cause you to drink or use other drugs. For your own good—indeed, for your own survival—you need to let go of your resentments and anger so that you can stop drinking and using other drugs and turn your will and life over to your Higher Power.

At this point, when you're willing to let go of resentment, you can begin to see the world a little differently. When you're all wrapped up in resentment, you become completely dominated by the world and by other people. As a result, what other people, institutions, and principles do determine who you are, what you think, and how you act. As long as you cling to your anger, other people will control your actions and your life. By reacting to others with resentments and anger, you put yourself in their power. And since resentment can be fatal, this means that the wrongdoing of others, whether real or imagined, has the power to end your life.

When we finally realized these things, twenty-some years ago, each of us thought, *Here I've been letting all these other people control me and determine who I am and what I think— and some of those people have been dead for twenty or thirty years!* We finally decided that we weren't going to let these people live in our heads anymore. We wanted a Higher Power, not other people, to direct our thinking.

Mastering Resentment

So we've seen that resentments must be mastered—but how? We can't wish them away any more than we can wish away our addiction to alcohol or other drugs.

p. 66, l. 32–
p. 67, l. 8 In the paragraph that begins at the bottom of page 66, the Big Book tells you exactly what you can do to master your resentments. What this paragraph says is that you should pray for the people you resent. Now, granted, this might not be easy, and it certainly won't be something you want to do. But remember what the Big Book said earlier—that recovery means the destruction of self-centeredness. The only reason that it's hard to pray for somebody you're mad at is because your self-centeredness is in the way.

But even if praying for someone you resent is the hardest thing in the world, you're better off praying for someone you can't stand than ending up drunk or stoned because of your resentment.

p. 552,
ll. 19-29 Lines 19-29 on page 552 of the Big Book repeat and reinforce this message. These lines also offer more specific instructions: Not only should you pray for the person or thing that you resent, but you should pray that he, she, or it receives *everything you want for yourself.* If you don't mean it, *do it anyway.* Do this once a day, every day, for two weeks, *no matter what happens.* At the end of two weeks, we believe your resentment and anger will be gone, and compassion and understanding will have taken their place.

This method may seem strange or even ridiculous at first, and it might be hard to do for the first few days. You might not be sure whom to pray to, or even if a Higher Power really exists. None of this matters. *Do it anyway.* No matter what you might think or feel about it, try it for two full weeks.

It really works. We have never seen this method fail—even for people who swore it wouldn't work.

p. 551,
l. 19–
p. 553,
l. 10 In fact, it even works where all other methods have failed. From line 19 on page 551 to the end of page 553, there's the story of an alcoholic in recovery who got rid of all her resentments except one. That resentment was against

her mother, and it seemed so huge and deep-seated that she feared it would drive her back to drinking. But she prayed daily for two weeks that her mother would receive all the things she wanted for herself. At the end of two weeks, the resentment had disappeared.

This woman used this method many times afterward, whenever a new resentment would arise, and it worked for her every time.

Why does this method work? It works because if you enter into communion with your Higher Power in concern for someone or something else, you can't resent that person or thing at the same time. Even if the concern is false at first, after a little while it starts to become real. Concern and resentment can't exist together; one pushes the other out. Eventually, it becomes impossible to resent the person you're praying for. After two weeks, the concern will have pushed out all of the resentment from your mind.

Here's something else about resentments: They seem huge and powerful when they're in your head, but once they're down on paper they no longer seem so huge or powerful. In fact, on paper a lot of resentments look downright stupid.

It has been our experience that 95 percent of all resentments look this way once they're written down. *These are the very same resentments that seemed completely reasonable and justified—and powerful—while they were in people's heads.* You can walk around with a resentment in your brain for twenty years, until it feels like it's a natural part of you. Then you put it down on paper, and it immediately looks stupid.

In fact, we've found that 95 percent of all resentments leave people once they actually put their resentments down on paper and see the truth about them. And we think that 95 percent of your own resentments will probably vanish, too, once you've written them all down, looked them over, and seen what they actually amount to. For those few resentments that do remain, you can get rid of them through prayer, using the method we described on page 104, paragraphs 2-5, of this book.

Getting rid of your resentments and anger, then, is nothing more than a simple two-step process. First, write down your resentments; second, pray. Ninety-five percent of your resentments will disappear because they look stupid; the other 5 percent will disappear through prayer.

What Replaces Anger

Maybe you've heard about the law of physics that says that nature abhors a vacuum. This means that whenever a vacuum is created, something will always rush in to fill it up. This is true of our heart and mind too. If your resentments disappear, you'll leave a vacuum inside of you that will have to get filled up with something else—and the only thing that can possibly fill it is the opposite of resentment.

As your resentments disappear, you'll begin to experience a little bit of love, patience, tolerance, and goodwill toward your fellow human beings. The more your resentments leave you, the more good feelings will flow in.

If a Higher Power dwells within us—and both of us are sure that it does—then love, patience, tolerance, and goodwill have always been a part of everyone's makeup. But maybe it wasn't as easy for you to tap in to these things before. If you're like most other alcoholics and addicts, you weren't able to feel them or use them because, in your search for money, power, prestige, sex, security, or whatever, you saw other people getting in your way, and you got angry at them.

But once your resentments have disappeared, the will of your Higher Power—which is love, patience, tolerance, and goodwill—can come to the surface. And soon, automatically, you'll begin to find yourself in possession of some peace of mind, serenity, and happiness.

CHAPTER THIRTEEN

More About Resentment

We haven't said everything we need to about resentments. The fact is that it won't do you much good to get rid of the resentments you have now if you don't know how to keep new ones from building up. After all, a lot of the people, institutions, and principles that once got you angry are still around, and some of them are going to keep on doing the same hurtful things. How can you keep from building up new resentments against them? And how can you avoid resenting any new people and things that might hurt you in the future?

Is there a way to be free of resentment altogether—not just free of particular resentments, but free of resentment, period?

Looking at Yourself

It probably comes as no surprise to you that the Big Book offers you a method for getting free of and staying free of resentment. This method is described in lines 14-24 on page 67. It works like this: Take each situation that caused you resentment or anger; then, disregarding everyone and everything else involved, look at what *you* did to cause the situation or to make it worse. What did you do that contributed to the problem? In each situation, how were you selfish, dishonest, self-seeking (inconsiderate), or frightened?

p. 67, ll. 14-24

It's easy to simply blame other people, institutions, or principles for everything. And it's just as easy to cover up our own role in something by saying, "It is all their fault." By transferring all of the blame to someone or something else, we avoid having to look at ourselves—and we can also avoid having to admit, "Well, actually I wasn't a total victim. I had something to do with it too."*

Sometimes we do selfish things that cause trouble for others, and they retaliate against us and cause us trouble too. By resenting them, though, we manage to distort the incident and cover up what we did that might have started the whole process rolling. When we replay the incident in our mind, the other person looks worse and worse and we look better and better. We make ourselves innocent victims in our mind, instead of honestly admitting that we contributed to the situation. In fact, sometimes when we look at the situation honestly, we'll discover that we actually caused the problem in the first place.

We need to say here that once in a while people do get hurt by things that are totally out of the blue, things they had absolutely nothing to do with. But if you're honest with yourself, you'll see that *most of the time* you were at least partly responsible for what happened to you. *This means that we all play a role in most of our own resentments.*

When the two of us first did our own personal inventories and looked over our resentments, we realized something totally unexpected: *Not one of our resentments was true!*

Now, they had looked true in our heads—but when we wrote them down, looked at them carefully, and tried to find the part we had played in each one, we realized that in every case we bore at least some of the blame. We also realized that what we thought had happened in each case wasn't what

---

* The exception we made back on page 99, regarding hidden sex, applies here too. You are not in any way responsible for any abuse, sexual or otherwise, that you suffered as a child or as an adult.

—EDITOR

had really happened. *We had used our resentments to alter what had happened in our memories and to transfer all the blame to other people.*

Drinking alcoholics tend to develop precisely these skills. We develop them because it's hard to live with ourselves if we honestly face what we do when we drink. But we don't have to face ourselves if we can focus on our resentments and use them to transfer the blame to other people, institutions, and principles.

In looking over our inventories, we were also amazed to find that *on our resentment lists there was not a single person who did something painful to us before we did something painful to him or her. In each case, we had done something to create a problem for that person first.*

This really blew our minds. Until then, we'd never really looked at ourselves and what we'd done to others. We only looked at what other people did, and resented them for doing it—no matter what we might have done that caused a problem for them. We never looked to see how we hurt them and how they, in turn, retaliated against us.

Recognizing Your Motivations

What we're suggesting you do now is look once more at each one of the resentments in your personal inventory, after you've completed it, going from the beginning of your list to the end. Disregard for the moment what other people, institutions, and principles did to you, and instead try to remember exactly what role *you* played in each situation. What did you do to cause a problem or make an already existing problem worse, either for yourself or someone else?

Start with the first resentment on your list. Let's suppose it involves your boss. Look at what you've written in all three columns; then think about what you might have done to cause a problem for your boss so that he or she retaliated against you. Be searching, thorough, fearless, and honest in your recollection.

We've noticed that all human beings share four basic character defects:

1. Selfishness
2. Dishonesty
3. Fearfulness
4. Inconsiderateness

All people react selfishly, dishonestly, with fear, or inconsiderately at times. Some people, however, show these defects more often and more deeply than others. And a lot of alcoholics and other addicts act in these ways habitually.

As you examine each situation in your inventory and discover what your own part in it was, ask yourself what motivated you to do it. Were you selfish, dishonest, afraid, or inconsiderate? Maybe you were motivated by two of these defects, or even all four.

Go down your whole inventory from beginning to end, recalling what your own role was in each situation and determining your motivation. For each item, to the right of column three, identify your motivation with an **S** (for self-ishness), a **D** (for dishonesty), an **F** (for fearfulness, fright), or an **I** (for inconsiderateness). If more than one of these motives apply in a situation, write down two, three, or even all four letters.

■ ■ ■

When you've gone through the entire inventory, put down your pen or pencil and look over what you've written to the right of the third column. What letter or letters appear most frequently? The more frequently a letter appears, the more the character defect it represents has affected your life—*and the more control it has over you right now.*

If the letter **S** appears often to the right of your third column, then you need to become less selfish and more generous and giving. If you've written a lot of **D**'s, then you need to become more honest. If you've written the letter **F** quite often, then you need to start practicing courage. And if you've written the letter **I** frequently, then you need to start being more considerate of others. The more frequently a particular letter appears, the more you'll need to work on the character defect it stands for as you put the remaining eight Steps into practice in your life. These four character defects will help us define the exact nature of our wrongs as we work Step Five. Each resentment we have is usually the result of a wrong we committed—and neither the wrong nor the resentment would exist if we had not been selfish, dishonest, afraid, or inconsiderate.

Fear of Change

At this point, you know a great deal about yourself and your resentments. You've decided that you want to be free from all resentment, both now and in the future. And you've realized just how important being free of resentment is to your sanity, stability, and sobriety.

What we're going to tell you next is extremely simple but absolutely true: *You can be 100 percent free of anything that anyone has ever done to you—or will do to you—if you are only willing, with the help of your Higher Power, to let it be so.* Up until now, you haven't been willing.

Here is something else that's just as simple but just as true: Your fear has blocked you from letting yourself be free of resentment. *The only thing that keeps you from being free of your resentments is your fear of living without them.* You are afraid of what might happen if those resentments disappear.

In other words, you're afraid of love, patience, tolerance, and goodwill—because these are what will take the place of your resentment when it's gone. You are afraid of serenity, happiness, and peace of mind as well—because they'll take the place of resentment too. *Most of all, you're probably afraid of having to change.*

If you have a fear that you don't want to get rid of, then you must be afraid of living without it. You may be using a fear to rationalize not doing something you really should do or, just as importantly, doing something you should not do. In that case, your selfish, dishonest, frightened, or inconsiderate character is holding you back.

In our next chapter, we'll look at your fear and show you what you can do to replace it with courage and hope.

CHAPTER FOURTEEN

Outgrowing Fear

By now you've realized two important things that might not have been clear to you before: First, if you want some peace of mind, some serenity, and some happiness, you're going to have to change. Second, the one and only thing that prevents you, or anyone else, from changing is fear.

The Nature of Fear

Most alcoholics and addicts who are still drinking and using are deeply affected by fear. In fact, as the Big Book says on lines 27-28 of page 67, fear touches virtually every aspect of their lives.

p. 67, ll. 27-28

This shouldn't be too surprising. After all, if you can't trust other people, and you won't trust a Power greater than yourself, and you can see your self starting to fail you, then you're going to be absolutely filled with fear, because you'll see that sooner or later you won't have anything at all to rely on, including yourself. So we need to look closely and carefully at fear and see what can be done about it.

First of all, let's be clear on what we want done about fear. We want to get rid of it. We want our fear removed from our mind.

Second, we need to understand what the biggest problem with fear is. *The worst thing about fear is that, like resentment, it blocks us off from our Higher Power.*

Remember that you are now carrying out the decision you made when you took Step Three. You decided to turn your will and your life over to the care of a Power greater than yourself. You want to get rid of the fear and resentment that control your thinking so that this Power can direct your thinking instead.

We should mention at this point that not all fear is harmful. Fear is a natural part of human life; in fact, it's necessary for our survival. We couldn't live a single day if we didn't have fear; we couldn't drive our cars, or walk across the street, or even eat a meal safely. We all would be constantly injuring ourselves—smashing up our cars, walking in front of moving buses, eating poisonous mushrooms, and so on. Fear gives us the common sense that keeps us alive. So a certain amount of fear can be beneficial in our life.

The problem comes when we use fear incorrectly, in the wrong places or circumstances, or at the wrong times. Used improperly, fear can become extremely destructive. It takes opportunities away from us and turns the control of our life over to other people.

Inventorying Your Fears

The best way to deal with your fears is to do exactly what you did with your resentments: Write them down, look carefully at them, understand what part you played in creating them, and recognize what your motives were for playing that part. In other words, you'll need to make an inventory of your fears, similar to the inventory of resentments you did in Chapter Twelve of this book.

To begin this inventory, take a sheet of paper and turn it on its side. You will be setting up three columns, much like you did before. The first column, which will take up the left third of the page, should be titled

I'm afraid of:

Column two, which will take up the middle third of the page, should be titled

The Cause

And column three, which will take up the right third of the page, should be headed

Affects my:

So, these will be the headings of your inventory chart for your fears:

I'm afraid of: *The Cause*   *Affects my:*

■ ■ ■

Then, get a pen or pencil and begin filling in your chart. As before, begin with column one (*I'm afraid of:*); fill in the entire column before moving on to column two. Think of all types of your fears—physical, mental, emotional, financial, whatever—as you list in column one all the people, institutions, and principles that frighten you. Take the time to think, search, and remember, and try to be as complete as possible. As before, if you later change your mind or want to add something, go ahead and make the change. Also as before, be as searching, thorough, fearless, and honest as possible. Leave an inch or so between items in column one so that you'll have plenty of room to fill in the other two columns.

Most people don't realize just how many fears they have or how much those fears dominate their thinking until they put them down on a piece of paper. We have fears about our job, our spouse, our children, the Internal Revenue Service, the police department, and so on. We have fears about what other people think of us and about what they might do to us.

Some of your fears will be rational, some irrational, some instinctive. You might have five or six, twenty or thirty, or well over one hundred fears. Write them all down. Use as many pieces of paper as you need to list them all.

■ ■ ■

Then move on to column two (*The Cause*). Start at the top and go through each of the fears on your list, one by one. What caused it? Something a person, an institution, or a principle did? Something you did? Something that happened to you years ago? Something that happened yesterday? Whatever it was, write it down.

Be simple and straightforward here; don't try to psycho-analyze yourself too much. Write down the clearest, most direct causes that you're aware of. We don't expect you to write down that you're afraid of the dark because your mother didn't change your diapers the right way when you were a baby. And if you simply don't know and can't figure out the cause for a certain fear, write down "don't know" in column two.

■ ■ ■

When you've worked column two from top to bottom, begin filling in column three (*Affects my:*).

You'll remember from Chapter Twelve of this book that people get angry when their social, security, and sexual instincts involving one or more of these eight basic life issues are threatened or interfered with in some way.

1. Self-esteem
2. Pride
3. Personal relationships
4. Material security
5. Emotional security
6. Acceptable sexual relations (sex that won't harm you or someone else and isn't in conflict with your values)
7. Hidden sexual relations (sex you have to hide from someone—your spouse, for example)
8. Ambitions (plans for the future)

It will likely come as no surprise to you that most of us can become *afraid as well as angry*, when one or more of these basic life issues, which determine our sense of *self*, get threatened or interfered with—or when we think one or more of them could get threatened or interfered with in the future.

In column three (*Affects my:*), you need to write down exactly which basic life issues are affected by your fears, that is, which ones you're afraid will get injured or destroyed. Go through column three from top to bottom, one fear at a time, and list whatever basic life issue or issues seem to be threatened in each case. Keep this book open to the list of the basic life issues on page 116—or, if you like, copy the list on a separate page. As with resentments, for most of your fears you can simply pick the appropriate basic life issue or issues from the list and write them down in column three. If more than one basic life issue is affected by a certain fear, write down all of those issues.

■ ■ ■

Once you've finished working column three, go back to the beginning of your inventory. As you did with your resentments, go through your list once more, one fear at a time. This time, however, forget about what other people, institutions, or principles may have done to you to make you feel afraid. Instead, look at what you might have done to hurt or threaten each person, institution, or principle. What did you do that might have caused a problem for them, so that they retaliated against you?

Then think about what motivated you to cause them trouble or pain in the first place. Was it selfishness, dishonesty, fearfulness, or inconsiderateness—or some combination?*

Then, pick up your pen or pencil again. As before, to the right of column three write in the letters **S** (for selfish), **D** (for

---

* Of course, if you were the victim of some trauma in your past, such as sexual or physical abuse, war, an accident, or a natural disaster, this doesn't apply. These fears will have to be worked out over time, perhaps with a counselor and certainly with help from your Higher Power.

—EDITOR

dishonest), **F** (for fearful, frightened), or **I** (for inconsiderate) to match the motive behind each action you took that hurt or threatened a person, institution, or principle. If more than one of the four motives apply in a situation, write in more than one letter.

Once you've finished noting your motives, your inventory of fears is complete. Put down your pen or pencil and take a short break.

■ ■ ■

Then look over your fears in column one again. Now, fears are just like resentments: They seem huge, threatening, powerful, and extremely real when they're in your head—but when you put them down on paper and look at them, most of them look silly or plain dumb.

If you're like most of the people we've worked with, when you look down your list of fears, they're going to seem trivial or stupid, and the great majority of them are going to disappear, just like that.

You can get rid of just about all of the rest through prayer, the same way you got rid of the rest of your resentments. We'll talk more about this in a moment.

After you've looked over column one thoroughly, look carefully at the rest of your inventory of fears. In particular, look at what you've written in the third column (*Affects my:*). Of the eight basic life issues listed on page 116—self-esteem, pride, personal relationships, material security, emotional security, acceptable sexual relations, hidden sexual relations, and ambitions—which ones appear most frequently in this column? The more frequently one of these basic life issues appears, the more fear you have about it, and the more you need to examine it closely and work on changing your fear.

The same is true for the letters to the right of column three: **S** (for selfish), **D** (for dishonest), **F** (for fearful, frightened), or **I** (for inconsiderate). The more frequently a letter appears, the more you need to work on correcting the character defect it refers to.

The Permanent Solution to Fear

Now that you've looked closely at your inventory of fears, you've seen just how many of them began with your own thinking and your own actions. This means that *if you can change your thinking and your actions, you can get rid of the source of your fears.* This is true even though you may have done nothing to cause the fear.

The opposite of this is also true: If you *don't* change your thinking and actions, and go on thinking and acting pretty much the same way you always have, the same familiar fears are probably going to keep coming back. Even though you can get rid of your fears through writing them down and through prayer, if there's no personality change, new fears are only going to rush in to take their place.

But if you can change your thinking and actions, you can start to *permanently* get rid of the fears that plague you. And instead of getting rid of each of your individual fears one by one, you can get rid of *fear itself.*

On page 68 of the Big Book, lines 3 through 27, there's quite a bit said about fear. At the end of this passage, there is a specific prescription for getting rid of all your fear: *Ask your Higher Power to remove fear, and ask that Power to show you what it wants you to be instead.* Remember, fear blocks you from your Higher Power, and it's that Power you want to get in touch with. p. 68, ll. 3-27

The last sentence of this passage is particularly important. It says that *as soon as you make such a prayer to your Higher Power, you begin to outgrow your fear. The results are immediate.* And the process of growth that you will have begun will continue as you continue working the Twelve Steps, until your fear is gone.

Back in Chapter Twelve of this book (page 104) we talked about a simple prayer for resentment, and now we have another simple prayer for fear. Both prayers are easy to practice and remember, and *both are 100 percent effective.* p. 66, l. 32–p. 67, l. 8

We said earlier that nature abhors a vacuum. As you outgrow your fear, something has got to take its place. That something is courage. As your fear disappears, courage begins to come to the surface.

So does faith. And, automatically, you will begin feeling better. You'll become less restless, irritable, and discontented. You'll feel less shame, guilt, and remorse. And you'll begin to feel some serenity and peace of mind.

As you continue to work the Twelve Steps, this serenity and peace of mind will grow. And soon you'll find that your life has been transformed from a life of fear and resentment into a life of happiness.

CHAPTER FIFTEEN

The Problem of Sex

There is one other area of your life that can block you from your Higher Power, and that area—sexual relations—can cause you to feel shame, guilt, and remorse. We think it's essential that people include the subject of sex in their personal inventories, because it seems that one of the fastest and easiest ways we can harm another human being is through our sexual conduct.

Once Chapter 5 of the Big Book has discussed resentment and fear, it moves immediately to the subject of sex. If you look carefully at Chapter 5, you'll see that when it discusses personal inventories, it focuses on three things: resentment, fear, and sexual conduct. These are the three areas you need to focus on when you make your own inventory.

The Nature of Sexuality

When it comes to sex, human beings are different from all other creatures on this planet. As far as we can tell, animals don't think about sex. They don't have the same powers of reasoning or ability to make choices and decisions as people do. They don't appear to think about having sex before they have it, or while they're having it, or after they've finished having it. When the right time or season arrives, the female and male find each other and mate, and that's that. For animals, sex is simple.

Animals don't have problems with sex because they don't become emotionally involved in it. Neither of us has ever seen a cow on a psychiatrist's couch talking about sexual dysfunction.

We human beings are different. We don't have to wait for the right time or season to have sex. We can have sex any hour, day, week, or month of the year that we want. We can have sex with as many people as we want to, as many times as we want, and in whatever positions we want. We can think about sex before we have it, while we're having it, and after we're done having it.

Our ability to think, reason, and make decisions causes us to become emotionally involved in sex. As a result of that involvement, sometimes we use sex to hurt one another. And unfortunately, sex can be used to hurt others faster, easier, and more deeply than just about any other means.

The Big Book's Stance on Sexual Conduct

The Big Book's discussion of sexuality begins with the last paragraph of page 68 and continues through line 22 on page 70. Take a look at the final paragraph on page 68 (continuing on page 69), which begins by stressing the importance of being sensible about the subject.

p. 68, l. 28–
p. 70, l. 22

p. 68, l. 27–
p. 69, l. 11

People have all kinds of extreme opinions about sex. Some say we should do it anywhere, anytime, and with anyone we please. Others say it's wrong unless you do it in a certain way and only with a certain person.

We want to make sure you understand what the Big Book's stance is on sexuality. This appears on lines 8-11 of page 69. It says that we will not be the *judge of anyone's sexual conduct*.

p. 69,
ll. 8-11

Then the Big Book comes right out and says that *everyone* has sex problems. In fact, we wouldn't be human if we didn't.

When the two of us first read those lines in the Big Book, we were enormously relieved. For one thing, we hadn't realized that everyone else had sex problems. We thought we were two screwed-up weirdos, two of the few people whose sex lives were less than perfect. We were also surprised; we had been sure that Bill W. and his cronies in Alcoholics Anonymous were getting ready to condemn us for what we'd done in the past, and we figured they were going to tell us what we were going to have to do and not do in the future. Well, we were wrong. The Big Book doesn't draw any lines where sex is concerned, nor does it tell you what's sexually acceptable and what's not.

What the Big Book *does* do, as we'll see in the next few pages of this book, is give you a way to look at your past sex life and see if you harmed other people through it. If you did, then the Big Book will help you develop a new sex life for the future—one that doesn't harm others, and one that you can live with without becoming restless, irritable, and discontented. It will be a sex life that won't result in fear, guilt, remorse, or shame.

Your new sex life might be with someone you've been involved with for some time and have hurt in the past. But it will have a different basis to it, a basis of honesty and compassion. This new sex life will help you to have peace of mind, serenity, and happiness in your life.

Inventorying Your Sexual Conduct

We said earlier that the Big Book's discussion of personal inventories was broken into three parts: resentment, fear, and sexual conduct. When you've done your inventory of resentments and your inventory of fears, you'll need to do a searching, fearless, truthful, moral inventory of your sexual conduct.

As before, start by taking a sheet of paper and turning it on its side. Divide it into three columns. Column one should take up the left third of the page; column two the middle third; and column three will take up the right third of the page.

Title the first column

I've hurt or threatened:

Title column two

What I did:

And call column three

The Cause:

So, these will be the headings for your inventory chart for your sexual conduct:

I've hurt or threatened: *What I did:*   *The Cause:*

These column headings are somewhat different from the ones you used in your resentment and fear inventories. We'll explain how these differences work shortly.

By now you've realized that taking inventory is not primarily a matter of figuring out who has hurt you. In fact, it's just the opposite.[*]

You want to figure out who *you* have harmed or threatened, how you harmed or threatened someone, and why you did it. That's where we suggest you start with your sexual conduct inventory. In column one *(I've hurt or threatened:)*, list all the people, institutions, and principles you've caused trouble for through your sexual behavior. As before, fill in this column from top to bottom before you move on to

---

[*] Again, if you have been sexually abused, either as a child or an adult, then, clearly, you were the one who was hurt, and these instances should not be placed on your sexual conduct inventory. The shame and fear that you have as a sexual abuse victim are not signs that you caused the problem. The person who caused the problem is the abuser, and you may want to seek professional help to heal the wounds of this trauma.
—EDITOR

column two. Leave about an inch between items in column one so that you'll have plenty of room to fill in the other two columns.

It is possible to hurt many different people in many different ways through sexual relations. We are not just asking you to list the people you were or are sexually involved with. For example, if you're married and have two kids, and you spend your evenings having sex with someone other than your spouse and your spouse finds out, then you've created problems for all kinds of people: your spouse, your children, the person you're having sex with, and, of course, yourself. If your secret lover has a family, then you're hurting those people too. One act of sexual misconduct can hurt many different people.

In your inventory, list everyone who you've harmed or threatened through your sexual activities, whether or not you've had sex with each of them, and regardless of each person's age or relationship to you. Then add all the institutions (such as your workplace, church, or school) and principles (that is, the values you once held about sexual behavior) that you betrayed by harming the people on your list.

Think carefully and try to make your list as thorough and complete as possible. If you come up with more items later, feel free to add them.

■ ■ ■

When you've finished filling in column one, begin working on column two, (*What I did:*). For each person, institution, or principle in column one, write down in column two what you did to cause each of them pain or trouble.

There are lots of different actions that might deserve to be listed in column two. Obviously, you can hurt someone by having sex with him or her, or by having sex with someone else instead of that person. But you can also hurt people simply by being demanding. Maybe you ignore your partner's desires and preferences and insist that he or she has sex with you on your terms or not at all. Maybe you hurt your partner by appearing cold and disinterested, and with-holding sex to punish him or her. Maybe you've created jealousy by flirting with someone in front of your spouse. All of these sorts of things should be listed on your second column.*

■ ■ ■

When you've finished working column two from top to bottom, begin filling in column three (*The Cause:*). Here we *don't* want you to say which events or other people caused you to do what you did. Instead, we want you to list what part of your self caused you to perform those actions. Which of your instinctive social, security, and sexual needs were threatened? In Chapters Twelve and Fourteen, we gave you a list of eight basic life issues that determine our sense of *self* and that are interfered with by resentments and fears: self-esteem, pride, personal relationships, material security, emotional security, acceptable sexual relations, hidden sexual relations, and ambitions. You won't need to use the two sexual issues—acceptable sexual relations or hidden sexual relations—in this inventory, since you already know that sexual behavior is going to be involved in each item on your list. The remaining six issues, then, are:

1. Self-esteem
2. Pride
3. Personal relationships
4. Material security
5. Emotional security
6. Ambitions

---

* If, in this list, you see a pattern of you having sexually abused others, then you need to start thinking now about how you're going to get help to break that pattern. If you've physically abused your partner(s) or forced people into sex—especially if you've raped someone or had incestuous relations or any sexual relations (whether physical, verbal, or visual) with children—make plans now to get professional help so you won't repeat this behavior. Sometimes drinking or other drug use masks other serious problems that need to be faced, dealt with, and solved in order to do a truly searching and fearless inventory.

—EDITOR

Most hurtful sexual conduct is based on the desire for one or more of these six basic life issues.

As you fill in column three (*The Cause:*) from top to bottom, keep these six issues closely in mind, and write them down wherever they apply. You'll probably find them coming up again and again. Keep this page open in front of you as you work column three, or write out these six basic life issues on a separate sheet of paper. Most of your entries in column three will be items from this list.

This surprises a lot of people at first. They think, *If I hurt someone through my sexual conduct, isn't the cause of my conduct my sex instinct? That's not even on the list!*

This may seem to be true at first—until you examine what it is you actually do. The fact of the matter is that *the sex instinct itself is rarely the cause of sexual behavior that hurts others.*

Our motivations are different from those of animals. It is rare that we feel sexual arousal and absolutely nothing else; usually it gets combined with other impulses. Once in a while the cause of a problem is pure sexual arousal, but if you look at your past carefully, you'll see that in the vast majority of cases, you were seeking something more than simply sex. You were trying to feel proud, or raise your self-esteem, or fulfill your desire for emotional security, material security, or a personal relationship.

Now, there's not the slightest thing wrong with wanting to feel proud, or trying to increase your self-esteem, or desiring material security, emotional security, or a personal relationship. If fact, all of these things are wonderful to have. *The problem comes when your desire to fulfill these basic life needs or issues causes you to hurt other people.*

For instance, a lot of people use sex to build up their self-esteem. The more people they can attract or have sex with, the bigger and better they feel. The problem is that in the process of making themselves feel bigger and better, they hurt those other people. Sex is involved, but it's not the cause of the problem. *The cause is the desire for greater self-esteem.* Sex is the mechanism or means that these people use to fulfill this desire.

Some people have sex so that they can have what they think will be a personal relationship with someone else. They may be lonely and want a companion, or maybe just some attention, so they have sex just so they can be with someone instead of having to be alone. Once again, sex is involved, but the real motivation is the desire for companionship, not the sex instinct.

Others use sex to bolster their pride. Maybe a man's spouse isn't behaving the way he'd like her to, so he says to himself, "I'll show her" and to "punish" his spouse, he goes out and starts sleeping with his spouse's best friend. He is not doing it for the sex; he is doing it for revenge, to fulfill his desire for pride.

All of these examples ultimately stem from a desire for something other than sex. As you fill in column three, think about how the desire for self-esteem, pride, personal relationships, material security, emotional security, and ambitions has affected your own sexual conduct.

■ ■ ■

Once you've completed column three, go back to the beginning of your inventory. Look at each item and ask yourself what motivated your actions. Was it selfishness, dishonesty, fearfulness, or inconsiderateness—or some combination?

For each item in your inventory, to the right of column three, list your motives. As before, use the letter **S** to stand for selfish, **D** for dishonest, **F** for fearful, frightened, and **I** for inconsiderate. When more than one of the four motives apply in a situation, use more than one letter.

Now put down your pen or pencil. It's time to look over this inventory and see what it all adds up to.

■ ■ ■

The very first thing we'd like you to recognize is that *your sex instinct is not the cause of your sexual problems. The causes are selfishness, dishonesty, fear, and inconsiderateness.** When these character defects direct your actions in pursuit of self-esteem, pride, personal relationships, material security, emotional security, or fulfillment of your ambitions, you end up causing pain and difficulty for others—and for yourself. Your sexuality may be what you used to pursue these ends, but it is not the source of your problems.

When the two of us first inventoried our own sexual conduct and realized that our sexuality was not the cause of our problems, we immediately felt much better. We had thought our sex drives were overpowering and abnormal, and we felt guilty about them—not to mention restless, irritable, and discontented. But when we looked at our inventories and realized what we'd been doing—using our sexuality to pursue other goals—then our sex drives didn't seem so all-powerful anymore, and we didn't feel so abnormal. We also realized that our selfishness, dishonesty, fear, and inconsiderateness were controlling us far more than our instinct for sex. We had thought that we were oversexed, but it turned out that we were actually undersecure and undercompassionate. We were trying to use sex to build up our sense of security and self-esteem.

Once we realized this, our sexual problems immediately started to diminish. The desire to keep doing the same things and create more problems became less and less. Our shame, guilt, and remorse began to disappear. And we found we weren't as restless, irritable, and discontented about sex anymore.

We think the same things will happen to you as you review your own inventory of your sexual conduct.

---

* The causes of sexual problems are selfishness, dishonesty, fear, and inconsiderateness *except* in cases of sexual disorders (including compulsive sexual behaviors), which are illnesses and require separate treatment. Both professional counseling and Twelve Step recovery groups are available for recovery from sex addiction.

—EDITOR

As you look over your inventory, take note of which of the six basic life issues—self-esteem, pride, personal relationships, material security, emotional security, and ambitions—appears most often in column three. The more often one of these appears, the more you desire it, the more it drives and controls you, and the more you need to look at it and work on it as you continue working the Twelve Steps.

The same is true of the letters to the right of column three. What letter or letters appear most frequently—the **S** for selfishness, the **D** for dishonesty, the **F** for fear, or the **I** for inconsiderateness? The letter or letters that appear most often will indicate the personality defects that have the most power over you right now. These are the defects that you need to pay the most attention to, and the ones that you need to work and pray to be rid of as you work the Twelve Steps.

Outgrowing Selfishness, Dishonesty, Fearfulness, and Inconsiderateness

Now that you have taken an inventory of your sexual conduct, what can you do to make changes to that conduct in the future? The Big Book gives you a clear, practical, easy-to-follow set of guidelines. These begin on line 25 of page 69 and continue through line 22 on page 70. They are: Be willing to make amends to the people, institutions, and principles you have harmed, provided we don't bring about more harm by doing so; avoid extreme thinking or advice; pray for sanity, strength, and the ability to do what is right.

p. 69, l. 25– p. 70, l. 22

In short, treat the sexual harm you've done like any other problem.

p. 70, ll. 18-22

In lines 18 through 22 on page 70, the Big Book explains exactly what to do when sex becomes particularly difficult to deal with. The answer is to throw yourself harder into helping others—not for what you think is *their* sake, but to get outside of your self for your own sake.

Getting outside your self and helping others is the ultimate method of escape from selfishness, dishonesty, fearfulness, and inconsiderateness. It can be used with any problem or desire, not just sex. If you have a serious problem in your own life, try helping another person. This really works—and you end up helping yourself.

When you're wrapped up in a problem, you're also completely wrapped up in your self. But when you help another person, you often get so involved that you're automatically taken out of your self. And once your self is forgotten, a Higher Power can take its place and start working in your life. *The way to escape from a preoccupation with self that blocks you from your Higher Power is to help another person.*

Completing Step Four

By now, you'll have done three personal inventories— one for your resentments, one for your fears, and one for your sexual conduct. In these inventories, you'll have listed most of the people, institutions, and principles you've hurt or threatened in your life. But maybe there will still be some that aren't listed in any of your three inventories. Maybe there will be some people, institutions, and principles you've caused trouble for in ways that have little or nothing to do with your fears, resentments, or sexual conduct.

To complete Step Four, you'll need to make a fourth and final inventory. You can call it a miscellaneous inventory. Include in it any people, institutions, and principles you've harmed or threatened in your life that you didn't include in any of your three previous inventories.

Set up this inventory in the same way you did the others. Turn a sheet of paper on its side. Make the left third of the page into column one; the middle third into column two; and the right third into column three. Title column one

I hurt or threatened:

Title column two

What I did:

And title column three

> *The Cause:*

So, these will be the headings for your miscellaneous inventory chart:

I hurt or threatened: *What I did:*   *The Cause:*

As before, work the columns one at a time, from top to bottom.

In column one (*I hurt or threatened:*), list all the people, institutions, and principles you've caused problems for, leaving an inch or so between each item.

■ ■ ■

In column two (*What I did:*), write down what you did that hurt or threatened each person, institution, or principle.

■ ■ ■

In column three (*The Cause:*), list the basic life issues that were threatened or interfered with, leading you to do what you did. You'll recall that the eight issues are:

1. Self-esteem
2. Pride
3. Personal relationships
4. Material security
5. Emotional security
6. Acceptable sexual relations (sex that won't harm you or someone else)
7. Hidden sexual relations (sex you have to hide from someone)
8. Ambitions

■ ■ ■

Finally, to the right of column three, list your motives: the character defect or defects that motivated your actions.

Use an S for selfish, a **D** for dishonest, an **F** for fearful, frightened, and an **I** for inconsiderate. Feel free to use more than one letter for each item.

■ ■ ■

When you've finished, look over your miscellaneous inventory. Which of the eight basic life issues appear most frequently in column three? Which of the four character defects are listed to the right of column three most often? What other patterns do you see? What else does the inventory tell you?

■ ■ ■

When you're done, you'll have finished with Step Four. You'll have completed a searching, thorough, fearless, and honest moral inventory of yourself. Please save these inventories for future reference; you'll be using them in most of the Steps and chapters to come.

When you're finished, you're ready for Step Five.

CHAPTER SIXTEEN

Into Recovery

The Big Book says over and over that faith can do for us what we cannot do for ourselves. We hope that by now you are convinced that a Higher Power can remove whatever self-will has blocked you from that Power. We also hope that you have begun to see the value of patience, tolerance, and goodwill toward your fellow human beings—and most importantly, the importance of putting these principles into practice in your daily life.

Confiding in Someone Else

The next Step is Step Five. In this Step, you admit to your Higher Power, to yourself, *and to another human being* the exact nature of your wrongs.

Since you've already worked Step Four, admitting your wrongs to yourself and to a Higher Power shouldn't be difficult. Your personal inventories already include a list of most of your wrongs. All it takes to own up to them and admit them to yourself and your Higher Power is some honesty and a little bit of courage.

The third part of Step Five is a little tougher. You need to talk about the wrongs you've done with another human being. Ideally, this should be someone who has walked the same road before you—someone who understands the Twelve Steps, the Big Book's inventory process, and what you're trying to do. This person can help you see things about yourself that you might not be able to see on your own, because this person can look at your life from the outside, and because some of his or her own experiences have been similar to yours. Your sponsor would probably be your best choice. If no such person is available, however, there are others familiar with Twelve Step recovery who can be helpful: many counselors, trusted friends, members of the clergy, etcetera. The Big Book (on lines 1 through 23 of page 74) makes several excellent recommendations for finding the right person to talk to.

p. 74, ll. 1-23

Notice in this passage that the Big Book suggests that you *not* go to someone who will be hurt or troubled by hearing your story. The person should understand, and perhaps be moved, but your confession must do him or her no harm.

p. 74, ll. 16-23

Confession is good for the soul, and you're going to feel a great deal better for doing it. But the main purpose of Step Five, as we see it, is to extract every bit of pertinent information about yourself that you can with the help of another human being. Your inventories from Step Four will get you most of the way toward making a full, open confession; your talk with another person in Step Five will take you the rest of the way there. We even suggest that you bring your four inventories with you (the inventories discussed in Chapters Twelve, Fourteen, and Fifteen) when you tell your story.

Your wrongs that you will discuss with another person will be those things that have blocked you from your Higher Power—resentments, fears, and the harm you've caused others. To get at the exact nature of each of your wrongs, you'll talk about what part or parts of your self is affected— social instinct (previously discussed as the basic human issues of self-esteem, pride, and personal relationships), security instinct (material and emotional), sex instinct (acceptable and hidden), or ambition—and which character defect caused it. Was it selfishness, dishonesty, fearfulness, or inconsiderateness?

Once you have worked Step Five, you'll notice the greatest personality changes taking place in yourself so far. The Big Book describes these changes eloquently on lines 11-21 of page 75. Here is where, at last, you begin to have a

p. 75, ll. 11-21

spiritual experience and know that your obsession with drinking no longer has to control your life.

Letting Go of Shortcomings, Defects, or Wrongs

The last paragraph on page 75 of the Big Book asks you, after you've worked Step Five, to review what you've done so far, to see if you've left anything out, and to be sure that you've been honest and thorough. You're asked to read over the first Five Steps once more and make sure you've worked them sincerely and completely.

p. 75, ll. 22-33

p. 59, ll. 9-18

Once you have fully worked Step Five, then you're ready for Step Six in which you acknowledge that you're entirely ready to have a Power greater than yourself remove all the defects of your character that you uncovered in Steps Four and Five.

The Big Book uses the term "wrongs" in Step Five, and the phrase "defects of character" in Step Six. In Step Seven, and other places in the text, the Big Book uses the word "shortcomings." At still other points in the text, the Big Book uses some other terms to mean "wrongs," "defects of character," and "shortcomings." We've been to Alcoholics Anonymous meetings where people have gotten into arguments over which character traits are "wrongs," which are "defects," and which ones are "shortcomings." We think that's missing the point. As far as we can tell, *all* these terms are saying exactly the same thing. In fact, throughout the Big Book, Bill W. often refers to the same thing using two, three, or four different terms, such as "defects," "faults," "mistakes," "personality flaws," "shortcomings," "wrongs," etcetera. We believe it's just a way of adding variety and avoiding repetition.

p. 59, ll. 18, 20, 21

It is interesting to us that simply becoming ready to have a Higher Power remove your character defects or short-comings is a separate Step (Step Six). It isn't until Step Seven that you actually ask your Higher Power to take away these shortcomings or defects. This is no accident. The Big Book recognizes that even though we might see and understand what all of our character defects or shortcomings are, we may not be willing to turn them loose quite yet.

Strange as it sounds, sometimes we'd rather sit in today's pain and suffer than take a chance on doing something different. We are used to the pain and know what it's like, and we've learned to deal with it in our own ways—but we don't know what the future will be like without that pain. So, in many cases, we'd rather suffer with what's familiar than take a chance on changing.

Another reason many of us don't want our character defects or shortcomings removed is that some of them are fun and exciting. They cause us and other people trouble, and they lead to restlessness and discontent instead of peace and serenity—but because they're fun and exciting, we're unwilling to let go of them.

Then some people worry that if a Higher Power removes all of their character defects, they won't have any personality left at all! But that's simply not how things work. You don't end up with a hole in your personality. Remember that nature abhors a vacuum. When your character defects or shortcomings disappear, other things will rush in to take their place: love, honesty, courage, unselfishness, the will of a Higher Power, and maybe even some peace and serenity. *Your character defects or shortcomings will be replaced by character strengths.* These will be so much better than anything you've ever had in your personality that you'll wonder why you didn't take this route earlier.

When you understand all of this fully, you are then truly ready to have your Higher Power remove all of your character defects or shortcomings—and you have taken Step Six.

Now you can take Step Seven, in which you humbly ask your Higher Power to remove all of these character defects or shortcomings.

At first, this Step may seem like just an afterthought to Step Six. But we learned that your Higher Power won't remove your character defects or shortcomings—or anything else—from your personality *unless you ask.*

The Big Book provides you with a prayer you can use for this purpose on lines 8-14 of page 76. We like this prayer because it's simple, straightforward, honest, and direct. But you don't have to use this prayer; if other words come to mind, use them. Feel free to say whatever springs naturally from your heart. p. 76, ll. 8-14

What most of us would like at this point would be for our Higher Power to zap us, take all our defects of character away from us in one fell swoop, and make us immediately pure as the driven snow. We think you can see already that this isn't how things work. Usually it's a slow, steady, gradual process.

One thing we've learned over the years is that our Higher Power can do things we can't—but this Power won't do things for us that we can do for ourselves. We can't remove our own defects of character; all we can do is ask our Higher Power to take them away from us. And that Power can and will take them away. But what *all of us* can do is practice living in a way that's different from the way we lived when we were ruled by our shortcomings. We can try to live according to some principles—the principles of unselfishness, honesty, courage, and considerateness.

Once you've asked your Higher Power to remove your selfishness, then with that Power's help you can practice unselfishness instead. Slowly, your old mental habits can die and be replaced by new ones. This will take time and work on your part, but with the help of a Higher Power and with what willpower you can muster while in your Higher Power's service, you can start becoming unselfish.

Once you've asked your Higher Power to take away your dishonesty, then with that Power's help and your sincere effort you can be honest. This might be difficult at first, but as your Higher Power slowly takes away your dishonesty and you practice being honest, your old habit dies and is replaced with dishonesty's opposite.

Once you've asked your Higher Power to remove your fear, then with the help of this Power and with your own willpower in your Higher Power's service, you can start to do those things you've always been afraid to do. And you can quit doing those things you were afraid to stop doing. After a while, you'll find courage beginning to replace your fear.

Once you've asked this Power to take away your inconsiderateness, then with your Higher Power's help and your own efforts and willpower in your Higher Power's service, you can start being considerate of others. Slowly, over time, through repeated practice, the old habit of inconsiderateness dies and the new habit of considerateness replaces it and becomes natural.

As you practice unselfishness, honesty, courage, and considerateness, something amazing will start to happen. The old you will disappear and die, and a new personality will take its place. And you'll find that this new personality and the new way of life that goes with it are far, far better than the personality and way of life you used to have.

Step Seven and Everyday Life

When the two of us first took Step Seven some twenty-plus years ago, we were concerned about how we'd be able to make a living if we had to be unselfish and honest and courageous and considerate. Since then we've learned that following the principles is a much better, easier, saner, and more comfortable way to live—and a much less stressful one too. For one thing, these principles don't cause any guilt or remorse. For another, you feel a lot, lot better about yourself—and you don't have to worry about getting caught doing things that land you in trouble. You will also get along a lot better with people.

Step Seven isn't something you just do once and get it over with. *You have to practice it regularly, on a daily basis.*

At first, this may mean making yourself do what you don't want to do. But as you establish this new pattern of thinking, acting, and living, you resist less and less, and eventually you *want* to do all those things you're doing. At this point, you don't have to *make* yourself do anything anymore. You just do what you know is right. And when you're not sure what's right, you ask your Higher Power for guidance.

As you continue to practice Step Seven and live according to the principles described in this chapter, you start responding with love and patience; these slowly become more and more a part of your personality. Your old ideas die and are replaced with better ones. You will eventually see revolutionary changes in your life. Your relationship with your Higher Power, with yourself, and with other people will become better.

CHAPTER SEVENTEEN

Making Amends

A Design for Living

By the time you've gotten to the Eighth Step using the Big Book as we've suggested, you've worked pretty hard on the first seven Steps, and great things will have begun to take place in your life. As you go further and continue to work the Twelve Steps, we think you'll come to see that the Big Book and the Steps are really a design for living. The Twelve Steps aren't a process that you do once; they're something that you bring with you, carry out, and practice day after day.

You will also see that the Twelve Steps boil down to one thing: *change*—changing your life, day after day. To remain free, you have to make changes constantly.

This design for living that the Big Book offers will work for anyone who wants to use it, regardless of a person's circumstances. We think this is because everyone has a Spirit, a Higher Power—some of us call it "God"—dwelling within each of us.

Now if this Power does dwell in each of us—and if you've thoroughly worked the Steps up to here, you'll be as sure as we are that it does—then the important question in life, the most basic question of all, is this: Do I live in harmony with this Power, or do I live in opposition and disharmony? Steps One through Seven have provided you with a way to find this harmony and live in it.

Steps One through Three put you in the right relationship with your Higher Power, a relationship where now your Higher Power, not you, is to be the director. Steps Four through Seven put you in the right relationship with yourself. In Steps Four through Seven, you could see what blocked you from your Higher Power, and you're doing something to eliminate character defects or shortcomings from your personality.

Now you're ready for Steps Eight and Nine, both of which give you an opportunity to live in harmony with your fellow human beings. They give you the chance to set things right with other people and to get rid of the fear, guilt, remorse, and shame that you might have felt in the past.

p. 59, ll. 22-23

In Step Eight, you make a list of all the people you've harmed, and you become willing to make amends to them

p. 59, ll. 24-26

all. In Step Nine, you actually make direct amends to these people wherever possible, except when doing so would hurt them or others.

By now, you've set things right with a Power greater than yourself. If you also can set things right with your fellow human beings, you're probably going to start feeling pretty good. And you're going to discover a way to live in which you can be sober, peaceful, happy, and free.

Starting from Within

The thing about setting things right with other people is that you've got to start from inside yourself. Starting on the outside doesn't work for most alcoholics.

Some professionals who work with alcoholics and addicts—psychiatrists, psychologists, and so on—say pretty much the opposite. They say, "Let's get this alcoholic a car and a job and a wife or a husband, and then this person will be able to stay sober." But from our observations and experiences, this approach simply doesn't work very well for people like us.

Back when the two of us were still drinking, there were plenty of times when each of us would have a car and a job and a wife, and we'd still end up drunk. Then each of us would have a car and a wife, but no job. So we'd run around and cheat on our wives, and we'd each end up with a car, no job, and no wife. Then we'd get drunk, wreck our cars, and we'd each end up with no car, no job, and no wife. We'd each stay sober for a while here and there, and get a new job or a new car, but soon we'd start drinking again and lose whatever it was we had managed to acquire while we were sober. We could never get the outside stuff straight until we first changed what was going on inside of us.

This is what the Twelve Steps are all about—changing what's going on inside of you—and with Steps Eight and Nine you can start to get rid of your fear, guilt, remorse, and shame that are all associated with the people you listed in your personal inventories—the people you hurt, threatened, or caused trouble for. Working Steps Eight and Nine gives you a chance to do something about all that hurt and trouble you caused. But you can't work Steps Eight and Nine until you've worked Steps One through Seven.

Willingness and Courage

The Big Book describes the process of working these two Steps on pages 76-84, beginning with the third paragraph on page 76. The first part of this paragraph deals with Step Eight: You make a list of all the people you've harmed and become willing to make amends to each of them.

p. 76, l. 15–
p. 84, l. 15

p. 76,
ll. 15-27

This is a very simple Step. In fact, you'll have done the first half of it already. Your personal inventories will contain a list of just about all of the people you've harmed. Then it's just a matter of being willing to make amends to all of them. If by now you've thought of some more people you've harmed, just add them to the list and analyze them as you did in your Step Four inventories.

Willingness is the key to Step Eight. If you're not completely willing to make amends, or if you think you're unable to or lack the courage, then the Big Book, on lines 24-25 of page 76, shows you exactly what to do: *You pray to your Higher Power, asking for willingness and courage, and you continue to pray until the willingness and the courage come.*

p. 76,
ll. 24-25

That is all there is to Step Eight—and willingness and courage are all you need to put the Step into practice in your life.

The Nows, The Laters, The Maybes, and The Nevers

Now, on your list there may be the names of people who you think you'll never be able to make amends to in a million years. *They will never understand,* you think. Or maybe you hurt them so badly that you're afraid they'll call the cops if you get within fifty feet of them.

Maybe there are some others who you just plain don't want to make amends to. They did some awful things to hurt you, and you're still feeling the pain. You don't want to give them the pleasure of hearing you admit that you hurt them also.

If you can hear yourself saying one or more of these things inside your head, we have a suggestion for you: Take that list of the people you've harmed and break it into four lists, putting each list on a separate sheet of paper. On List One, write the names of all the people you're willing to make amends to right now. Let's call these people *The Nows.*

■ ■ ■

On List Two, put the names of the folks you know you'll make amends to sooner or later. You might not be very happy about making amends to them, but you know that it makes sense, and you're going to do it in the foreseeable future. We'll call these people *The Laters.*

■ ■ ■

List Three will be *The Maybes,* the people you think you *maybe* can bring yourself to make amends to—but you're not sure.

■ ■ ■

List Four will be *The Nevers,* those people you don't ever plan to make amends to, no matter what happens.

■ ■ ■

Put these lists in a little pile, in order, with List One on top and List Four on bottom.

■ ■ ■

You can start with the first name on List One: Go and make amends to that person, and then go make amends to the second person on the list, and so on, until you've finished with all The Nows.

By the time you're finished with The Nows, we think you'll be ready for The Laters; so you can then make amends to the people on List Two, starting with the first person on the list and working your way down.

By the time you've done The Laters, you ought to be ready to make amends to all of the people on The Maybes list, one by one.

We'll bet that once you're done with The Maybes, you'll have the courage and the compassion to go out and make amends to those people you thought you'd never be able to face.

We didn't come up with this strategy ourselves. It was given to us by our Alcoholics Anonymous sponsors when we were first asked to take Steps Eight and Nine. At first, each of us said to our sponsors, "Hey, there's no way I can make amends to some of these people." Our sponsors suggested this strategy, and said, "Listen, we think if you go about it this way you'll be able to make amends to every one of these folks." They turned out to be 100 percent right.

A lot of people get hung up on Steps Eight and Nine, or try to avoid them or block them out entirely because they're not willing to make amends to everyone they've harmed. They let the two or three most difficult names on their lists drag them to a screeching halt.

But nowhere in the Big Book does it say you have to make amends to everyone all at once. It can be a gradual, steady process in which you make amends to one person at a time. And nowhere in the Big Book does it say you have to begin by making amends to the people you most despise, or the ones you've hurt most deeply. You are free to start with the easiest names on your list and gradually work your way through to the toughest. Each person you make amends to will help give you the courage and the compassion to make amends to the next person on your list. But if at any point your courage or compassion fails you, pray to your Higher Power for help and guidance.

As you begin making amends, and as you see the benefits that come from making them, you'll become more and more willing to make amends to everyone you've harmed.

Making Your Amends in Person

Step Nine is the act of actually making amends. The Big Book discusses Step Nine on pages 77-84, beginning with line 18 on page 77. The purpose of making these amends is to further help you get rid of the fear, guilt, remorse, and shame that have become associated with the people you've hurt over the years.

p. 77, l. 18–
p. 84, l. 15

Notice that the Big Book doesn't just say, "Make amends." We think it's important that Step Nine asks you to make *direct* amends. Usually this means making amends face to face.

We have seen over and over that making amends face to face is the best way, and that it usually yields the best results. The Big Book doesn't say that you can't write someone a letter or call a person on the phone, but we strongly believe that one should make amends in person wherever possible, face to face, one on one.

We have heard about one fellow in AA who asked his sponsor if he could make his amends by mail. His sponsor said, "Yes, if you harmed them by mail."

Unless you meet with someone face to face, you're never quite sure you've done your utmost to make amends to that person. And it's important that you do your utmost. Step Nine doesn't work if you try to do it halfheartedly or with half-measures. You've got to make your best sincere effort—otherwise you're not really working Step Nine at all.

If you write someone a letter or make a phone call, there may still be some doubt in your mind as to whether you're making your best sincere effort. Maybe you're really trying to avoid having to fully and honestly face up to that person. But if you sit down with somebody, eyeball to eyeball, there will be no doubt in your mind that you've done your utmost. There will also be no doubt about how your attempts to make amends are received, because the person will be right there in front of you.

Sometimes, of course, it's just impossible to meet someone face-to-face. Maybe she lives a thousand miles away; or the only way to reach him is through a post office box; or she just plain refuses to meet with you. When an in-person meeting just can't happen, then go ahead and make a phone call or send a letter.

But we want to stress that you will be astounded by how well meeting somebody in person works. There's something about face-to-face contact that opens up compassion and goodwill and forgiveness in other people. Often, when somebody starts working Step Nine and sits down to make amends with someone he has injured, the other person says, "Well, you know, I've wanted to sit down with you for a long time myself. I've done you wrong, too, and I need to apologize to you for it." Sometimes the other person winds up becoming a good friend.

Here is one of the key elements of Step Nine, and one of the things that makes it so wonderful: If you go to someone to make amends, but she won't accept you or see you (maybe she throws you out of her home or office), *you've still done your part.* You've done your best to make amends, so *you don't have to worry about that person anymore.* If someone won't accept you, that's that person's business, not yours. You've tried your best to set things straight.

Here is something else that's great: You don't have to be afraid of that person anymore. After all, she's already done her worst to you by refusing to talk to you. And if she's already done her worst and you've done your best, then there's no reason to be afraid of her anymore, and the fear associated with her should disappear.

Repaying Your Debts

p. 78,
ll 14-25 Lines 14-25 on page 78 in the Big Book deal specifically with repaying people to whom you owe money. The word *direct* in *direct amends* means "open and straightforward," but it also means "proportionate and equal." You need to make your amends in direct proportion to what you owe. If you owe someone one thousand dollars, to make direct amends to that person you need to repay him one thousand dollars, and maybe some interest too—let your conscience decide that.

So part of Step Nine involves going to people to whom you owe money and saying, "Here's how much I owe you, and I want to make some arrangements for paying it back."

A lot of alcoholics don't see a reason or point in doing this. But there's a spiritual maxim that says that the only way to get rid of guilt and remorse is through making full and equal restitution. People have believed and followed this maxim for a couple of thousand years, and it's as true now as it has ever been.

Now what most of us would probably like to do is wait until we get together all the money we owe someone in one lump sum, so that we can go in, all puffed up and grandiose, slam down a wad of bills on the desk, and say, "Here's all your damn money." But let's face it, you're not going to do that, and you almost certainly haven't got the money to do it just after you sober up.

Nowhere in the Big Book does it say, "You have to pay back every penny you owe everyone right this minute." That's probably just plain impossible. But you do need to be willing to repay each debt in full over a reasonable period of time, and you need to go to a person openly and honestly, and say, "Let's make arrangements so that I can take care of this debt." Tell each person what your financial situation is and how much you can pay her—five dollars a week, fifteen dollars a month, whatever. Be honest and specific. Be honest about your limitations too. If someone wants you to pay him back at the rate of one hundred dollars per month and you know you simply can't, then say so straightforwardly—and tell her how much you *can* pay.

If you owe someone or some institution money, either of them would rather have a small amount every week or month than nothing. You may be surprised how most of your creditors will be glad to work with you under this kind of arrangement. You may be even more surprised at how much better you'll feel as soon as you start making this restitution.

One of the great things about this part of Step Nine is that you don't have to pay back all the money before you can start feeling better about your debts. As soon as you start repaying people, the fear associated with those people and your debts to them will disappear. You don't have to worry about coming into contact with those people anymore because you've already talked with them and worked things out.

We know someone from AA named Dan, who has been sober now for about thirty years. Dan is only five feet, two inches tall, but when one of us recently asked him how he was doing, he said, "I feel about eight feet tall. This is the first time in my life when I don't owe somebody something because of what I stole from them in the past." It took Dan twenty-nine years to repay all his debts—but he did it, and he is proud of himself for it. We believe he deserves to feel that way.

We can't tell you how great it feels to be able to walk down the street anywhere in the world and not have to worry about running into someone who we owe money to, or who wants to get back at us, or who's angry at us, or who wants to arrest us, hit us, or serve us with a subpoena.

So once you've made your amends, you're going to feel a lot better about yourself, about other people, and about your whole life. But that's not the reason why you make amends. You do it because it's the right thing to do. Even more, you do it because you have to, because it's a vital part of your recovery program. In fact, the question isn't really whether you want to make amends or not. The question is, "Can I find peace of mind and happiness and stay sober if I don't make amends?" We believe strongly that the answer is no, you can't.

p. 78,
ll. 23-25

The Big Book says this in a slightly different way on lines 23-25 of page 78. It says quite straightforwardly that we must lose our fear of creditors if we want to stay away from alcohol. It doesn't say, "It's a good idea to lose your fear of creditors," or "You really ought to lose your fear of creditors." The Big Book says that *we must lose this fear to ensure that we stay sober.*

When to Not Make Amends

p. 83,
ll. 19-28

Now let's take a look at lines 19-28 on page 83. This is an important paragraph, and it's based on the part of Step Nine that says you should make direct amends wherever possible *except when doing so would harm other people.*

The fact is that there are some amends you can't make at all. Maybe the people you need to make amends to are dead. In other cases, trying to set things straight will only cause more pain to the people you've hurt before. Or the people may not be aware of everything you did, and if you confess it all to them you may only hurt them even more. Then you'd have to turn around and make amends to them for having made amends. None of us has the right to clear our own conscience at the expense of someone else. If making amends to certain people is only going to hurt them or is going to do them more harm than good, don't do it. Admit to yourself and your Higher Power the exact nature of your wrongs against those people, and let those people be.

Lines 19-28 on page 83 of the Big Book explain that some wrongs can never be fully righted. Some amends may genuinely have to be postponed or avoided. *But what's important is that you're sincerely willing to make those amends right now, even though actually doing so might not be possible.* You need to say, "I'd set things straight right now if I could." If you can say this to yourself and mean it, then you've done your part and your utmost, and you don't have to worry about the situation or be afraid of the person any further.

What About Going Back to Those Who Turned You Away?

When you make amends, we think you'll be surprised at how many people will let you come in and talk to them, and we think you'll be pleased and even amazed at how many of them will accept you and your offer of amends. Some of them will be even downright friendly. If you approach people honestly and humbly, most of them will respond with acceptance and even goodwill.

But some won't, and a few never will. Some will throw you out or refuse to have anything to do with you. It's important for you to understand that *this is their problem, not yours.*

You may be tempted to go back to those who turned you away and beg them to forgive you. But you don't need to do this—*in fact, you shouldn't.* The Big Book is very clear on this issue. On lines 25-28 on page 83, it says that we should be sensible and tactful, *not* groveling. You should stand up to make amends, never crawl. If someone won't accept your amends, simply say to yourself, "I've done the best I can do; now I can move on." And you don't have to worry about this person or be afraid of him or her anymore.

p. 83, ll. 25-28

One Person You Need to Make Amends To You Shouldn't Forget About

That's yourself. And the best thing you can do to make amends to yourself is relieve yourself of the fear, guilt, remorse, and shame associated with your past. You can make amends to yourself by working Step Nine fully and sincerely, and by earnestly proceeding with the Steps that follow.

The Big Book's Promises to You

Before we move on to Step Ten, we want you to look over what you've done in Steps One through Nine. We would like you to begin doing this by reading a passage from the

A Program for You

p. 83, l. 29–
p. 84, l. 11 Big Book. It begins with line 29 on page 83 and continues through line 11 on page 84. It's a list of promises that the Twelve Step program, the AA fellowship, and Bill W. all make to you. Please read (or reread) them now.

■ ■ ■

We believe the fulfillment of these promises is the direct result of getting right with your Higher Power in Steps One through Three, getting right with yourself in Steps Four through Seven, and getting right with your fellow humans in Steps Eight and Nine. Steps One through Nine are a design for living that really works.

If you have worked the first nine Steps fully and sincerely, then every one of these promises will come true for you. They will come true as the result of your own commitment, your hard work, and the love of your Higher Power. *These promises never fail.* They will always come true if you work for them—not sometimes, not most of the time, but every time. The Big Book guarantees this in lines 14-15 on page 84.

p. 84,
ll. 14-15 We guarantee it too.

CHAPTER EIGHTEEN

The Spiritual Dimension

Everything in our universe is either growing or dying. Something is either going forward or going back. Nothing ever stays the same.

Most of us can find a young tree near where we live and notice how it grows. It will grow year after year, becoming more beautiful each year, until one day it quits growing. And the day it quits growing it begins to die. Eventually, it dies and turns to earth and dust, returning to its source.

By working Steps One through Nine you've succeeded in transforming your life. But if you try to stay where you are without growing anymore, you'll start dying—not physically, but emotionally and spiritually. Eventually, you'll slip back and start having difficulty with people again. That will cause trouble in your mind, and resentments and fears will start showing up once more. These resentments and fears will begin to block you off from your Higher Power, and eventually you could start telling yourself that you can safely drink or use again, which, if left unchallenged, will surely bring your physical death as well.

So you need to find a way to keep yourself growing. The last three of the Twelve Steps are designed to help you continue your spiritual growth.

A Lifetime of Spiritual Growth

On lines 13-24 of page 25 in the Big Book, Bill W. talks about "a fourth dimension of existence" that he and the p. 25, ll. 13-24 other early Alcoholics Anonymous members discovered through their spiritual experiences. Once you've completed Steps One through Nine, you have already recovered in the first three dimensions of life—the spiritual, mental, and physical. You can now begin to live in this fourth dimension as well if you continue to practice the Twelve Step program.

Most of us have never experienced or thought about such a dimension. Before the two of us stopped drinking, neither of us could even begin to imagine it. We didn't know you could live without being mad. We didn't know you could live without being afraid. And we didn't know you could live without hurting other people. But now we not only see this dimension clearly, we live in it—and the result is indescribably wonderful. You have to feel it and experience it to know what it is. But we have felt it, experienced it, and known it ourselves, and we want you to as well.

Working Steps Ten through Twelve will enable you to have this experience.

Some people say that the last three Steps of the Twelve Step program are "maintenance Steps." By this, they mean that Steps Ten, Eleven, and Twelve keep you from slipping back into old, destructive ways of thinking, acting, and living. We agree that this is one of the purposes of the final three Steps—but we don't agree with the term "maintenance Steps." We don't think you can merely maintain anything. You have got to either grow or regress.

Steps Ten, Eleven, and Twelve will help you to keep growing spiritually and emotionally. Certainly, they keep you from slipping backward—but they also help you to keep moving forward. And you can use them to keep moving forward and growing for the rest of your life.

Let's look at the Big Book's description of Step Ten, which runs from line 16 on page 84 through line 23 on page 85.

In Step Ten you continue to take personal inventory, and whenever you are wrong you promptly admit it. You also continue to grow in effectiveness, understanding, and spirit.

p. 84, l. 16–
p. 85, l. 23

You don't work Step Ten for a day, a week, or ten years—you work it *for the rest of your life.* Working Step Ten means continuously working Steps Four through Nine on a daily basis.

We have noticed that some people shrink down Step Ten and try to make it shorter and easier than it really is. They think it just means that if you hurt someone during the day, you should make amends, and that's that. But the Big Book shows that Step Ten means far more than that. Step Ten involves all of the six immediately preceding Steps (Steps Four through Nine)—and it means not just making amends, but living a life of the Spirit.

According to the Big Book, Step Ten means continuing to watch for selfishness, dishonesty, resentment, and fear (Step Four). When these crop up, we ask God to remove them (Steps Six and Seven), discuss them with someone immediately (Step Five), and make amends quickly if we have harmed someone (Steps Eight and Nine). And you must ask your Higher Power daily how you can best serve that Power's will instead of your own. As the Big Book says in line 23 on page 85, this is the proper use of your will.

p. 84,
ll. 23-27

p. 85,
ll. 18-20

p. 85, l. 23

The Return of Sanity

All of this adds up to something a great deal more than just admitting when you're wrong and then making amends. It means growing into a fourth dimension of living, the dimension of Spirit. Perhaps, most of all, it means sanity. Because by now, having worked Steps One through Ten, your sanity will have returned. You will no longer be interested in drinking alcohol or in practicing your other addictions.

As you continue to work Step Ten in your life, you'll see your character defects become smaller and smaller. Your relationship with God as you understand God will become better and better. So will your relationship with your fellow human beings and with yourself. And at long last you'll have taken responsibility for your own behavior.

The two of us now know, as the result of working the Twelve Steps, that we are responsible for the way we feel and for what we say and do. Before we started working the Steps, especially Step Ten, we didn't know this—we just automatically reacted to people and things. But today we know how to stop ourselves from merely reacting. We know how to stop blaming others.

If one of us is fouled up today, it's his fault—not someone else's. Once in a while one of us will choose to be fouled up, or angry, or afraid. But when we do, we know exactly what we're doing and that we're doing it by choice. That takes all the fun out of it, of course, and pretty soon we simmer down.

Yet More Promises

In the last chapter we pointed out the promises the Big Book makes on the bottom of page 83 and the top of page 84, and we explained how these promises will always come true if you work for them.

p. 84, l. 30–
p. 85, l. 12

Well, just three paragraphs later, beginning with line 30 on page 84 and continuing through line 12 on page 85, the Big Book makes some more promises. So long as you stay in good spiritual condition and work Step Ten regularly and earnestly, each of these promises will come true as well. They have for us.

When the two of us were first recovering and working the Twelve Steps, something strange happened. We were going through the Big Book carefully and working the Steps to the best of our abilities—and somewhere between page 45 and page 85, our obsession to drink disappeared. In fact, the very urge to drink disappeared. We believe that our Higher Power took that urge and that obsession away from us.

We said earlier that in order to recover, you need to find a Power greater than yourself that would solve your alcohol or other drug problem—not help you solve it or enable you to solve it, but *solve it*. Somewhere as we were in the middle of working the Twelve Steps, our Higher Power solved our problem for us by removing it from our minds. We were no longer obsessed with alcohol. Our sanity had returned.

Only a Power greater than ourselves could remove our obsession with alcohol. If we had to fight that obsession on a daily basis, we'd end up doing exactly what we used to do twenty-odd years ago: get drunk.

But, thank God, we don't have to fight that obsession because a Higher Power removed it from us and replaced it with something much better than alcohol ever was.

This is the real miracle of this program given to us in the Big Book, *Alcoholics Anonymous*.

CHAPTER NINETEEN

Prayer and Meditation

After you've worked Step Ten for a while and all of the Big Book's promises have come true in your life, you may think to yourself, *There's no way that things can get any better than this.* If you're not careful, you'll really believe this thought and stop growing spiritually. The fact is that things can and will get better still—provided you continue with your efforts and keep working the Twelve Step program.

In lines 13-23 on page 85 of the Big Book, Bill W. lets us know that if we rest on our laurels we're headed for trouble. We have got to use our willpower to serve and follow our Higher Power. Otherwise, we can slip backward.

p. 85,
ll. 13-23

Gaining Knowledge and Power

We just love pages 84 and 85 of the Big Book. If you're like most alcoholics and addicts, by the time you actually picked up the Big Book, alcohol or your other addictions and your obsession with it had long ago taken away your sanity. Then when you worked Step Three, you made a decision to give up your will. If you work the program thoroughly and sincerely, by the time you reach page 84 your sanity will have returned. And then, one page later, you get your will back as well.

p. 84, l. 16–
p. 85, l. 31

p. 84,
ll. 31-32
p. 85,
ll. 18-23

Now that you have your will and your sanity back, you can't stop with Step Ten. If a Higher Power dwells in every human being and has all knowledge and all power, then it stands to reason that each of us has within ourselves all the knowledge and power that we'll ever need to take care of any situation. If you had a way to tap into the knowledge and power of God, as you understand God, then you'd be able to deal with any set of circumstances that might arise.

As it turns out, there are two ways, not one, to tap into this knowledge and power: through prayer and through meditation.

When people read about the importance of prayer and meditation, a lot of them draw a blank at first—or else they come up with a big question mark. Or maybe they remember the prayer that they used to use over and over when they were drinking: "God, get me out of this damn mess, and I swear I'll never do it again!" That's a typical alcoholic's prayer. In fact, that was pretty much the extent of our own prayer lives before we came to Alcoholics Anonymous. As for meditation, we knew nothing about it at all.

Before we started working the Twelve Steps, we never used prayer as a way to receive the will of a Higher Power into our lives. It never occurred to us to even want to receive that will and carry it out. Our idea of prayer was to approach God with a list of our petty wants. We would ask for this thing and that thing, and we'd try to sway God's will to suit our own.

Now this wasn't a very healthy prayer life, and as a result we had a lot of trouble with prayer when we first came into AA. We asked questions like, "How does my Higher Power know what I want?" We learned that our Higher Power isn't interested in what we want—but that Power knows exactly what each of us needs. And in the twenty-plus years since we started working the Twelve Steps, this Power has given us far more than we imagined we could possibly have.

If we had made a list of every one of our petty wants back then, and if every single one of them were fulfilled, they wouldn't even begin to compare to what our Higher Power has actually given us. We've learned that we don't need to give this Power a list of our petty wants. All we need to do is pray for our Higher Power's will and direction.

And this is exactly what Step Eleven is all about. It tells us to seek through prayer and meditation to improve our conscious contact with God, as we understand God, praying only for the knowledge of God's will and the power to carry out that will.

p. 59, ll. 29-32

The Big Book's Plan for Prayer

For someone who hasn't had a lot of experience with prayer and no experience at all with meditation, this may seem pretty difficult to understand, let alone put into practice, at first. So let's look at what the Big Book has to say about prayer and meditation.

The instructions for working Step Eleven begin on line 32 of page 85 and continue through line 7 on page 88. Now is a good time to reread these pages so that they're fresh in your mind as we talk about them.

p. 85, l. 32– p. 88, l. 7

■ ■ ■

We need to remember that these pages were written by a man who wasn't a spiritual giant—not a minister or a philosopher or a religious scholar. He was an alcoholic stockbroker and speculator who'd been sober for about three and one-half years. And here he was, wrestling with an awesome responsibility as he tried to write something for his fellow alcoholics, most of whom had been spiritually bankrupt for years.

So, Bill W. wasn't an expert on prayer and meditation and, actually, we're glad he wasn't. A lot of theologians and other experts speak right over people's heads, and especially over the heads of people who have been spiritually bankrupt. But Bill W. doesn't speak over anyone's head. He gets down to basics and writes very simply and directly.

These are some of the most amazing pages of the Big Book to us. There are hundreds of books written about prayer, and probably hundreds more about meditation. But this man, this ordinary stockbroker, writes not a volume, not even a whole chapter, but less than three full pages about prayer and meditation, and in these few pages he lays out a complete plan that has enabled millions of people to live spiritual lives.

He does it very skillfully, very beautifully. Bill W. was a salesman, and he was extremely good. Since he knew very little about prayer and meditation, he didn't try to teach them to us, thank God. Instead, he laid out some very valuable suggestions and a daily plan of action. We would like to study these pages with you now and see how this plan works.

Learning to Pray and Meditate

We have already pointed out that if you learn to pray and meditate in the right way, you can tap into all of the knowledge and power that comes from a Higher Power. This knowledge and power can be an inner source of your strength, and with that strength you can enter another dimension of living—called the fourth dimension in the Big Book—and operate on God's will and power instead of your own.

The Big Book doesn't teach you *how* to pray or meditate; instead, it gives you a way to teach yourself. If you can practice the Big Book's daily exercises and suggestions (described on pages 86-88) day in and day out, then sometime in the future you'll have taught yourself prayer and meditation.

p. 86, l. 5–
p. 88, l. 7

The first suggestion, which begins on line 5 of page 86, deals with what you can do at night, before going to bed. The very next paragraph covers what to do when you wake up. The paragraph after that covers what you can do when faced with indecision. The remaining paragraphs on page 87, and continuing on page 88, tell us what to pray for, and then offer some other practical suggestions and advice.

If you use the suggestions on these three pages for daily prayer and meditation in your life, in a short time you'll be able to see a Higher Power's direction for you. And eventually you'll develop a sixth sense for knowing that direction in your life.

This may sound mystical and idealistic, but it's absolutely accurate. In fact, *we've never known these suggestions for prayer and meditation to fail for anyone who applies them sincerely.*

Learning to Arrive at the Right Thought, Answer, Decision

We would like to share with you some of the things that have happened for us over the years as a result of following the Big Book's suggestions for prayer and meditation.

We learned to let go, relax, and take it easy.

We learned that we can turn everything over to our Higher Power.

We learned that this Power has all knowledge and all power and about ten thousand answers for every question either of us might have. And when we have a question that needs answering or a problem that needs solving, we can simply turn it over to this Power and relax. We don't have to come up with an answer on our own right away. We relax and take it easy, and after a while the right answer will come to us. Sometimes it comes from inside of us; sometimes we find it in other people. But the answer—the right answer—always comes.

We're more mindful than we used to be. We realize that our Higher Power speaks through other people. In fact, our Higher Power speaks through all people.

When we first came to AA, we would only listen to certain people. Now we realize that our Higher Power doesn't speak through just "the smartest" or "most successful." We try to be open and listen to everyone.

We mentioned that we learned to relax and take it easy. This doesn't mean we lie down and clear our minds of all thoughts. What we mean is that we ask our Higher Power for the right thought, answer, or decision. Then we go on about our business, and that frees our minds from having to come up with the right thought, answer, or decision on their own. It also frees our minds to focus on other things. At the same time, it gives our Higher Power a chance to answer us because our minds are now occupied with other thoughts instead of being focused entirely on the question or problem. Instead of struggling with something and jamming all outside frequencies in the process, we let go of the struggle and let our Higher Power answer us.

It's amazing to us how this works. And it does work. If you get your mind on something else, later on the right thought, answer, or decision will come along. But as long as you're struggling to get at the answer yourself, your Higher Power can't get into your head because you've completely filled it up with trying to get the answer by yourself.

Learning to Put Inspiration to Work

We also want to mention hunches and inspirations. We've all had hunches, and we all know that we can't run our life entirely on them because they seem to come sporadically, only when they want to.

You can't control them. But hunches and inspiration can become working parts of your mind if you follow the Big Book's suggestions on pages 86-88. And as you practice prayer and meditation in your daily life, inspiration will become more and more a natural part of your thinking.

p. 86, l. 5–
p. 88, l. 7

Now some of what we've talked about in this chapter may be hard to do, especially at first. The Big Book's suggestions for prayer and meditation will take lots of practice on your part—unending practice—in order for you to become familiar and comfortable with them. But you can accomplish this. Both of us managed to accomplish it, and we were a couple of the sorriest alcoholics you ever saw.

Once we were completely lost in life. Now, however, we realize that the only things we need today and tomorrow and the day after that are the directions of a Higher Power and the power to carry those directions out. Above all, this is what the two of us have learned from Step Eleven.

CHAPTER TWENTY

A Vision of Awakening

We have arrived at Step Twelve, at Chapter 7 of the Big Book, and at the last chapter of this book. When you've diligently worked the program, as we've described it up to here, you've made it through the first eleven Steps, and you've had the Big Book's biggest promise fulfilled in your life: You have had a spiritual awakening.

Step Twelve begins with these words: "Having had a spiritual awakening. . . ." This is stated not as a hope or a wish, *but as a fact.* Step Twelve begins by promising you that if you apply the previous eleven Steps in your life and use the kit of simple spiritual tools the Big Book provides, you will have a spiritual awakening. Not "might have" or "should have" or "will probably have"—*will have.* p. 60, l. 1

Characteristics of a Spiritual Awakening

What exactly is a spiritual awakening? According to Appendix II of the Big Book, it's a personality change sufficient to bring about recovery from alcoholism. p. 569, ll. 1-5

In Bill's W.'s book, *Twelve Steps and Twelve Traditions,* he says that there are as many different kinds of spiritual awakenings as there are people in Alcoholics Anonymous. But all spiritual awakenings have certain things in common.

First, you're able to see and feel things that you could never see or feel before. For example, today both of us feel love for our fellow human beings. Before we started working the Twelve Steps we didn't know what love was. We had love, sex, attraction, and attachment all mixed up. Today we understand what love is. It's compassion, patience, tolerance, goodwill, and understanding. Love is wanting other people to have what you have.

Once you've had a spiritual awakening, you will know things you never knew before. Today both of us know that our Higher Power is kind and loving and that this Power stands ready to help any human being anywhere in the world. All anybody has to do is be ready to give up self-will and turn to God, as each person understands God, for knowledge and power. Before, all the two of us knew about God was hellfire and brimstone.

After you've had a spiritual awakening, you'll be able to do things you never could do before. You'll be able to live and get along with your fellow human beings. You'll be able to deal with them openly and honestly as equals, without resentment, fear, guilt, or remorse. You'll be able to live your life with serenity and peace of mind, instead of restlessness, irritation, or discontent. Most important, you'll be able to stay sober. As a result of the Twelve Steps and the love of our Higher Power, both of us have been able to do all of these things for many years.

So according to the Big Book's criteria, both of us have certainly had spiritual awakenings. When you've worked the first eleven Steps fully and sincerely, then just as surely you'll have such an awakening as well.

Sharing Your Recovery with Others

When you've had a spiritual awakening, what are you supposed to do with it? The Big Book answers this question in Step Twelve, which says:

> Having had a spiritual awakening as the result of these steps, we tried to carry this message to alcoholics, and to practice these principles in all our affairs.

What is this message that you are to bring to the alcoholic or other addict who still suffers? *That you've had a spiritual awakening as the result of the Twelve Steps.* This is the only real message that we have to offer to anybody. It is the central message of the Big Book, and it's the central message of the book you're reading now.

Why should you take this message to other alcoholics or addicts? Because you're an expert on the disease you're recovering from. Nobody really knows what it's like to be an alcoholic except an alcoholic. Nobody knows more about recovery from alcoholism than a recovering alcoholic. And a recovering alcoholic has a stronger message of hope to take to other alcoholics than anyone else. The same is proving true for those who are living this program and recovering from other addictions.

In fact, everything you are and do as a recovering person can bring hope and light, and perhaps even recovery, to another alcoholic or addict who is still drinking or active in his or her addiction.

Our Higher Power (the two of us use the name God) has always worked with people through people. God very seldom talks to people face to face, one on one. What God usually does is work *through* people. We carry the message that God wants carried to other alcoholics. In doing this, we have the opportunity to avert death by alcoholism in countless people.

Chapter 7 of the Big Book, "Working with Others," tells you exactly how to deliver this message to others. It gives you clear, specific instructions on what to do and what not do. When you read and reread Chapter 7, we hope you'll take what it says to heart and carry out its instructions and suggestions.

■ ■ ■

The final part of Step Twelve is *"to practice these principles in all our affairs."* We believe "these principles" are nothing more than the Twelve Steps. On page 60, lines 10-11 of the Big Book, we're told "the principles we have set down are guides to progress." If we look back on pages 59 and 60 to see what had been "set down," we find the Twelve Steps.

P. 60, ll. 10-11

A Few Last Words

We would like to leave you with a couple of final thoughts on the Twelve Steps.

First, keep in mind that no one, literally no one, has been able to maintain perfect and constant adherence to the Twelve Steps and the spiritual principles presented in the Big Book. We are all imperfect human beings, and at times we fail or fall short of our goals. Bill W. knew this, and he specifically urges us in the Big Book not to get discouraged. The Twelve Steps are for our guidance, not for 100 percent perfect obedience.

p. 60, l. 6

If we could practice the Twelve Steps in all our affairs, all the time and everywhere we go, then we could have peace of mind, serenity, and happiness twenty-four hours a day. Practicing them all the time is probably impossible—but it's a goal worth striving for.

We claim spiritual progress, not spiritual perfection. We're not perfect, we're not going to be perfect, and we shouldn't expect ourselves to be perfect. Honesty, sincerity, effort, and a genuine willingness to change are what count.

All of this is really up to you. When you follow to the best of your ability the program of recovery as it's given in the Big Book, you've got all the tools you need, and you know what to do with them and how to practice them. No one else can practice these principles for you. You have to work them yourself.

The Big Book says that what it offers are only suggestions. We realize that each of us knows only a small amount. Your Higher Power will constantly disclose more to you as you continue to practice the Twelve Steps.

Abandon yourself to God as you understand God. You do that in Steps One, Two, and Three. Admit your faults to God and to your fellow men and women. You do that in Steps Four, Five, Six, and Seven. Clear away the wreckage of your past. You do that in Steps Eight and Nine. Give freely of what you find. You do that in Steps Ten, Eleven, and Twelve.

Join us.

We shall be with you in the fellowship of the spirit. May God bless you and keep you.

THE TWELVE STEPS
OF ALCOHOLICS ANONYMOUS[*]

1. We admitted we were powerless over alcohol — that our lives had become unmanageable.
2. Came to believe that a Power greater than ourselves could restore us to sanity.
3. Made a decision to turn our will and our lives over to the care of God *as we understood Him.*
4. Made a searching and fearless moral inventory of ourselves.
5. Admitted to God, to ourselves, and to another human being the exact nature of our wrongs.
6. Were entirely ready to have God remove all these defects of character.
7. Humbly asked Him to remove our shortcomings.
8. Made a list of all persons we had harmed, and became willing to make amends to them all.
9. Made direct amends to such people wherever possible, except when to do so would injure them or others.
10. Continued to take personal inventory and when we were wrong promptly admitted it.
11. Sought through prayer and meditation to improve our conscious contact with God *as we understood Him,* praying only for knowledge of His will for us and the power to carry that out.
12. Having had a spiritual awakening as the result of these steps, we tried to carry this message to alcoholics, and to practice these principles in all our affairs.

---

[*]The Twelve Steps of A.A. are taken from *Alcoholics Anonymous,* 3rd ed., published by AA World Services, Inc., New York, N.Y., 59-60. Reprinted with permission of AA World Services, Inc.

THE TWELVE TRADITIONS
OF ALCOHOLICS ANONYMOUS*

1. Our common welfare should come first; personal recovery depends upon A.A. unity.

2. For our group purpose there is but one ultimate authority—a loving God as He may express Himself in our group conscience. Our leaders are but trusted servants; they do not govern.

3. The only requirement for A.A. membership is a desire to stop drinking.

4. Each group should be autonomous except in matters affecting other groups or A.A. as a whole.

5. Each group has but one primary purpose—to carry its message to the alcoholic who still suffers.

6. An A.A. group ought never endorse, finance or lend the A.A. name to any related facility or outside enterprise, lest problems of money, property and prestige divert us from our primary purpose.

7. Every A.A. group ought to be fully self-supporting, declining outside contributions.

8. Alcoholics Anonymous should remain forever non-professional, but our service centers may employ special workers.

9. A.A., as such, ought never be organized; but we may create service boards or committees directly responsible to those they serve.

10. Alcoholics Anonymous has no opinion on outside issues; hence the A.A. name ought never be drawn into public controversy.

11. Our public relations policy is based on attraction rather than promotion; we need always maintain personal anonymity at the level of press, radio and films.

12. Anonymity is the spiritual foundation of all our Traditions, ever reminding us to place principles before personalities.

---

*The Twelve Traditions of A.A. are taken from *Alcoholics Anonymous,* 3rd. ed., published by AA World Services, Inc., New York, N.Y., 564. Reprinted with permission of AA World Services, Inc.

Index

Other titles that will interest you . . .

The Big Book Workbooks

created by James Hubal and Joanne Hubal
based on material from A Program for You

Through clear discussions of each Step and suggested writing or drawing exercises, these workbooks offer a place to begin building a new design for living. Used in conjunction with the Big Book, *Alcoholics Anonymous*, these three workbooks provide an excellent resource for working the Steps the first time, or any time.

A Guide to the Big Book's Design for Living with Your Higher Power
A Workbook for Steps 1-3
Order No. 5421   36pp.

A Guide to the Big Book's Design for Living with Yourself
A Workbook for Steps 4-7
Order No. 5422   52pp.

A Guide to the Big Book's Design for Living with Others
A Workbook for Steps 8-12
Order No. 5423   39 pp.

The Big Book Workbooks
Set of three
Order No. 0827

A Program for You (audio album)
A Guide to the Big Book's Design for Living

The oral tradition of AA comes alive on these four audio cassettes, featuring the authors of *A Program for You*. They guide you in an exploration of the Big Book, bringing to light how the program serves as a design for freedom from addictive living. Listening to these tapes will make you part of the most exciting Big Book meeting you've ever attended. Four cassettes, 90 min. each.
Order No. 5638

For price and order information, or a free catalog, please call our Telephone Representatives.

HAZELDEN EDUCATIONAL MATERIALS

Pleasant Valley Road • P.O. Box 176 • Center City, MN 55012-0176

1-800-328-9000   **1-612-257-4010**   **1-612-257-1331**

(Toll Free. U.S., Canada,   (Outside the U.S.   (FAX)
and the Virgin Islands)   and Canada)